Marjorie F. Crick.

1965.

Marjorie F. Crick.

The Drawing Room at Southill, Bedfordshire.

REGENCY FURNITURE

1795–1830

MARGARET JOURDAIN

REVISED AND ENLARGED BY

Ralph Fastnedge

COUNTRY LIFE LIMITED

2–10 TAVISTOCK STREET COVENT GARDEN LONDON

First published in 1934
Revised and enlarged edition 1948
Revised edition 1949
Revised and enlarged edition 1965
Printed in Great Britain
R. MacLehose and Company, Limited

© *Country Life Limited 1965*

CONTENTS

ILLUSTRATIONS

FOREWORD

Margaret Jourdain, the author of this work (first published in 1934 under the title *Regency Furniture, 1795–1820*), died in April, 1951. She had been acknowledged for many years past a leading authority on English furniture and decoration, and had written extensively within that field of study. *Regency Furniture* was a pioneer study which she revised and enlarged in 1948, and revised again in 1949; and it has remained a classic for more than a quarter of a century.

This (the fourth) edition is again enlarged. The period covered by the term 'Regency' has now been extended to 1830, to include the reign of George IV, and additions to the text include sections on Thomas Sheraton's *Cabinet Dictionary* and *Encyclopaedia* and George Smith's *Household Furniture*, The Gothic Taste, The French Taste and The Later Regency. The number of illustrations, of individual pieces of furniture and also of designs drawn from contemporary pattern books, has been increased, but some of the material appearing in the earlier editions has necessarily been omitted.

1965   RALPH FASTNEDGE

ACKNOWLEDGMENTS

The illustrations of furniture from the Royal Collections are reproduced by gracious permission of Her Majesty The Queen (Figs. 8, 11–12, 39–41, 66–7, 73, 97, 98–100, 102, 152, 166, 212).

Illustrations which appeared in the 1949 edition, and which have been retained, were acknowledged as follows. The original provenance is here given, although much of this furniture may have changed hands in recent years.

Admiralty House, Whitehall, London, 156; The Viscount Allendale, Bretton Park, 116, 155, 203; Alveston House, 224; Balls Park, 202; Bank of England, 80; Major General Sir Wilkinson Bird, 223; Boodle's Club, 227; The Earl of Bradford, Weston Park, 87, 109, 111, 124; Browsholme Hall, Yorkshire, 74; The Earl of Caledon, Caledon, Ireland, 44, 96; Henry Channon, Esq., 42–3, 45; Crawley House, Aspley Guise, 234; Denston Hall, 210, 233, 241; Dixton Manor, 33; Lord Doverdale, 132; Ralph Dutton, Esq., Hinton Ampner House, 115, 120, 125–6, 138, 177, 206; Sir John Hall, 205, 215; Halnaby Hall, 228; Headfort, Ireland, 3; Sir Henry Hoare, Bart., Stourhead, 34, 78, 86, 133; Hotspur, Richmond, 129; Lord Huntingfield, Heveningham Hall, 180; Basil Ionides, Esq., Buxted Park, 38, 230; Sir Roderick and Lady Jones, 75, 107, 225, 242; Julians, 32; Lord Leconfield, Petworth, 196; Town Hall, Liverpool, 13, 89, 117; Lord Methuen, Corsham Court, 235; The Earl of Morley, Saltram, 26; Captain Musker, 164; Formerly at Normanton Park, 172; The Marquess of Northampton, Castle Ashby, 119, 171; The Duke of Northumberland, Syon House, 113–14, 237; Ragley Hall, 239; H. Goodhart Rendell, Esq., 82; The Duke of Richmond, Goodwood House, 35, 122; J. F. Roxburgh, Esq., 208, 217; 20, St James's Square, 127; The Earl of Sandwich, Hinchinbrooke, 31, 168, 176; F. Seddon, Esq., 131; The Earl of Shaftesbury, St Giles's House, 140, 146, 189, 214; Mrs Stileman, 134, 145, 153, 157, 246; The Thomas-Stanford Museum, Brighton, 101, 220; Ronald Tree, Esq., Ditchley, 105; Mrs R. Tree, 142; Trinity College, Oxford, 200–1; Robert Tritton, Esq., Godmersham Park, 173; The Victoria and Albert Museum, 19–21, 108, 139, 165, 186–7, 247; James Watson-Gandy-Brandreth, Esq., Buckland Newton, 18; The Duke of Wellington, 158, 191, 248; Humphrey Whitbread, Esq., 236; S. Whitbread, Esq., Southill, 2, 4–7, 9, 110, 123, 141, 143, 174–5, 213, 218; Mrs Clement Williams, 37, 192; Clough Williams-Ellis, Esq., 71; Wimpole Hall, 240; Mrs Gordon Woodhouse, 92; Lord Yarborough, Brocklesby Park, 79, 88, 193.

Grateful acknowledgment is made also to the owners of pieces additionally illustrated and for the use of photographs:

Ayer & Co. (Antiques) Ltd., Bath, 10, 55, 57, 150, 167, 181, 184–5, 188, 198; The Bank of England, London, E.C.2, 238; E. T. Biggs & Sons, Ltd., Maidenhead, 137, 162, 194; H. Blairman & Sons, Ltd., London, W.1, 46–7, 135–6, 144, 149, 226, 232; Brighton Corporation, 72; Browns of Liverpool, 65; MM. Jean Chelo, Paris 8e, 28; Chichester Antiques, Ltd., Chichester, 121, 148; M. Harris & Sons, London, W.C.1, 95, 159, 169; Martin Hutton, Battle, 51; Jeremy, Ltd., London, S.W.3, 147; Trustees of The Lady Lever Art Gallery, Port Sunlight, 76–7, 90, 151; Prides of London, Ltd., London, S.W.1, 50, 83, 91, 93, 178; Sotheby & Co., London, W.1, 69; The Victoria and Albert Museum, London, S.W.7, 54, 84, 207, 249; Trustees of The Wallace Collection, London, W.1, 68; Temple Williams, Ltd., London, W.1, 22, 52, 56, 103, 112, 128, 154, 160–1, 179, 182, 204, 245.

The colour plates are reproduced from photographs in the possession of the publishers, taken by kind permission of Major Simon Whitbread (Frontispiece); Brighton Corporation (I); the Director and Secretary, Victoria and Albert Museum (II), and the Master of the Merchant Taylors' Company (III).

Thanks are due also to Miss Joan Newton, and to the many people who have supplied information and who have helped in various ways in this revision.

PREFACE TO SECOND EDITION

The term Regency as now applied to the decorative arts in England overlaps the short period when George, Prince of Wales, was Regent, and covers all the work in the new classic style a decade before the institution of the Regency in 1811, and after his accession as George IV in 1820. It is a more acceptable title than 'English Empire', for the English classic is not a close version of, but an offshoot from, the French Imperial style. The new style was not derived from the taste of the Prince of Wales, whose leanings were towards oriental lacquer and lavish gilding, and the overcharged and dazzling splendour at Windsor Castle was, it is said, 'His Majesty's taste'.[1]

The style was for long termed 'English Empire', a description which indicates its debt to France. The style of Louis XVI was the last to follow in architecture the quest of recapturing the spirit of antiquity, and of using and adapting its ornament by a process of selection. Revolutionary France[2] led the way in a new classical movement, aiming at a close reproduction of ancient monuments, or when this was not possible, of such portions of these as could be adapted.

The French version of the classic style, which reached its zenith under Napoleon, became part of the artistic heritage of the European countries which had formed the Napoleonic Empire — Holland, Italy and Spain; and Sweden and Germany adopted it with little modification.

The aim of the leading artists and decorators was the union of architecture, decoration and furnishing. 'Furniture is too closely connected', according to Percier and Fontaine, arbiters of taste in France, whose *Recueil de décorations intérieures* was widely read, 'for the architect to remain indifferent to it. Construction and decoration are in close relation, and if they cease to appear so, there is a flaw in the whole.' In the French classical revival it was admitted that the rigid imitation of antiquity was impossible, and Fontaine recognised that a compromise was necessary. Symbols from Roman antiquity were used as relevant to the Napoleonic present; the nation's pride showed itself as the figures of winged victories; the sphinxes served to recall the delusive successes of 1798 in Egypt; and Roman weapons and shields summoned up associations of 'ancient virtue'.

In England the style can be seen in being in Sheraton's first book of designs, *The Cabinet-Maker and Upholsterer's Drawing-Book* (1791–4), and is well marked in his *Cabinet Dictionary* which was issued in 1803. The debt to the French Empire style is not so large as in other countries of Western Europe, and certain designers, for instance, Charles Heathcote Tatham and Thomas Hope, studied antiquity at first hand in Italy. The most

gifted exponent of the early phase of the style was the architect Henry Holland, who altered and enlarged Carlton House for the Prince of Wales, 'improved' Woburn for the Duke of Bedford, recased and redecorated much of Althorp for Lord Spencer, and altered and decorated Southill for Samuel Whitbread.[3] He borrowed elements from the French Directoire style, and employed a number of French craftsmen, painters and metal workers who found employment at a standstill in France during the Revolution and the Directory. After Holland's death in 1806, design stiffened in the grip of an uncompromising classicism, borrowing from the marble and metal remains preserved and excavated in Italy.

Samuel Rogers's home in St James's Square was entirely 'Grecian', and one of the most striking features of the house was its large collection of Greek vases.[4] In Sir Edward Lytton Bulwer's house in Charles Street, one of the drawing-rooms was a facsimile of a chamber he had visited at Pompeii, with vases, candelabra, chairs and tables in the Pompeian taste;[5] Thomas Hope's interiors at Duchess Street, London, were a consistent archaeological fantasy recorded in his *Household Furniture and Interior Decoration* (1807). Numerous pieces of Roman bronze furniture and parts of furniture have been preserved, especially from Pompeii, including couches, low stools, tripods and lamp-stands, dating chiefly from the time of the Emperors. The designers of the Regency transformed these forms of Roman bronze and marble into *wooden* furniture.

The Regency period was subject to swift and changeful currents in design. Many pieces of furniture, in the words of the author of the *New Circle of the Mechanical Arts* (1819) were 'daily falling into disuse, while others are introduced which, for a time, are considered indispensably necessary for our comfort'. The novelty and ingenuity of patents and forms is constantly emphasised. The later phase of Regency design is less happy, and as it developed, there was a greater profusion of ornament,

---

[1] C. B. Wollaston, who saw Windsor Castle in 1828, noticed the 'dazzling splendour of the gilding, which seems to be much overdone', and Mr W——ville said it was 'His Majesty's taste' — *Journal of Mary Frampton*, p. 337.

[2] The dates of French political changes are:
Directoire, 1795–9.
Napoleon, first Consul, 1799–1804.
Napoleon, Emperor, 1804–15.

[3] Holland's work at Carlton House dates from soon after 1783, on the Prince's coming of age. In 1789 he 'improved' Woburn; and his alterations to Althorp were completed in 1790.

[4] Clayden, *Early Life of Samuel Rogers*, Vol. I, pp. 448–9.

[5] G. Church, *Mayfair and Belgravia* (1892), p. 102.

13

and an increasing bulk which allowed more surface to be enriched.

Regency design has had an influence upon modern work. 'They were the modernists of a hundred and thirty years ago', as Mr Christopher Hussey writes, 'and were actuated by the same impatience with triviality that has stimulated their modern successors, seeking the same remedies in solidity and simplicity to which Parisian *ensembliers* have had recourse.'[1] There is the same accent on what Hope aimed at, 'breadth and repose of surface', 'distinctness and contrast of outline', and 'the opposition of plain and enriched parts'. Strictly speaking, 'Regency' might be applied only to those innovators, but in practice it is also used to cover a type of furniture which is not 'new' or classical, but is a simplification of the eighteenth-century tradition.

Not a little of the interest of 'Regency' work lies in the similarity of outlook in the designers of that period and their modern successors. 'In each case the designers have been actuated by the same desire: to evolve a form which shall owe as little as possible to precedent and custom, but satisfy by its compactness, sanity and sound use of materials.' In each case the designer accepts the advantages of machine-simplification.[2]

London, 1947   MARGARET JOURDAIN

---

[1] Christopher Hussey, *Country Life*, December 7, 1929.
[2] *i.e.* in Regency furniture, the use of cast metal mounts.

The Greek Revival

ENGLAND in the early nineteenth century was dazzled by that 'point of light in history', ancient Greece; and even before the opening of the century, Charles Heathcote Tatham writes to Holland of the interest in Greek architecture which is gaining ground in England. In almost all new buildings Grecian members and ornaments were 'so prevalent as to obtrude themselves upon the notice of the most superficial observer'.[1] Greek ornament was to be found in the houses of men of taste; and when Samuel Rogers bought a house in St James's Square in 1802, 'Greek vases dotted the house; much of the furniture was modelled on the same classic source, and the staircase was decorated with a frieze copied from a famous original among the Elgin marbles.'

The leading architect in this transitional period was Henry Holland who, beginning in the Adam tradition, developed his style in the direction of the French version of classicism, and shows in his interior decoration and furniture a delicacy of invention that cannot be matched in the work of any other architect of this period. In a book of office drawings in the library of the Royal Institute of British Architects there are sketches for furniture, mirrors and pier tables, and a bookcase for the library at Woburn, and also drawings for bookcases for Debden Hall (1796). In the alterations and redecorations undertaken by him for the Whig noblemen of the day — Lord Palmerston at Broadlands, and Lord Spencer at Althorp — the same sane taste is visible which marks his work at Carlton House.[2] During the last phase — the decade before his death — he was 'the most open of architects then working, to French fashions. It was his Gallican — or as the Tories considered, Jacobin — bias that made him so acceptable to the Carlton House coterie'.[3]

Holland was a brilliant decorative artist whose work is often a 'perfect combination of the requirements of eye and use'. There was in most of what he designed an assured distinction only to be matched in the contemporary French decorative arts. His style is to be seen in the furniture at Southill designed for Samuel Whitbread, and also in furniture made for Carlton House during the last few years of the eighteenth century. The degree of his responsibility for the design of furniture at Carlton House, Southill, Althorp and elsewhere remains uncertain: his designs were never published, and those that have survived, identified as his, are few. Nevertheless he must have been actively concerned with the furnishing of these houses. Closely associated with Holland is Charles Heathcote Tatham (1771–1842) (brother of the cabinet-maker Thomas Tatham), an architect who had been sent by Holland to make drawings in

Rome of classic detail to be used at Carlton House. The fruits of his stay are contained in a celebrated and very influential work first published in 1799 and entitled *Etchings Representing the Best Examples of Ancient Ornamental Architecture* (Fig. 1). To him the writer of the Architectural Publication Society's *Dictionary* (1842) assigns a large share in the rise of the Anglo-Greek style.

Holland, who was engaged to transform and redecorate the existing house at Southill inherited by Samuel Whitbread in 1796, was paid in 1801 £200 as 'commission on furniture', and one or two drawings for architectural fixtures at Southill are preserved (Frontispiece).[4] 'The Southill accounts show an average yearly expenditure on furniture over the whole period from 1796 to Samuel Whitbread's death in 1815 of some £1,000. In the peak period, 1800 to 1802, the yearly average was two and a half times as high. From 1803 to 1808 it dropped far below the average.'[5]

In the furniture of this early period, the material employed is a dark wood, such as rosewood, kingwood or mahogany, which throws up the finished brass or ormolu mounts and mouldings (Figs. 2–5). The mouldings are sometimes emphasised by the juxtaposition of ebonised bandings. The detail, such as the anthemium and the acanthus spray, is drawn from Greek ornament (Fig. 6). The French influence is traceable in certain forms, such as the shelved commode (Fig. 5) and the slender ormolu colonnettes at the corners of the rosewood china cabinet (Fig. 2). In the lady's writing-table (which dates from the first years of the second decade of the century), the rectilinear severity of the supports is relieved by the carved and gilt Greek detail of the feet and the ormolu ornaments applied to the supports (Fig. 7).

While Southill has the richest equipment of furniture made under Holland's jurisdiction, there are pieces originally at Carlton House in which there is the same characteristic abstemiousness and effective Greek detail. The closest approximation to the Empire style is to be seen in the rosewood bookcases in the Regency Room, Buckingham Palace (Fig. 8); the ormolu mounts in these, and in two larger bookcases by the same firm, are unusually varied, and it is probable that some French founder, such as Dominique, was employed. The book-

[1] Busby, *Villas and Country Houses* (1808).
[2] Henry Holland was architect to the Prince of Wales until his death in 1806.
[3] *Country Life*, November 9, 1929.
[4] Sketch book in the R.I.B.A. Library.
[5] Note from Mr Humphrey Whitbread.

Fig. 1. 'Antique Chimera in basso relievo of white marble, a fragment at Rome'; etching, from Tatham's Ancient Ornamental Architecture (1799), Plate 40.

Fig. 2. China cabinet, of rosewood, with slender colonnettes and ornamental applied mounts of ormolu. By William Marsh, c. 1800.

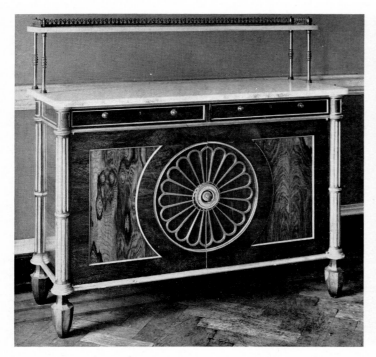

Fig. 3. Rosewood commode, decorated with ormolu mounts; from Headfort, in Ireland. (There is a commode of similar design at Southill, for which ebony is used as a contrasting wood, but it is not fitted with a gallery.) Height (to top of gallery), 4 ft ½ in.; length, 4 ft 2 in.

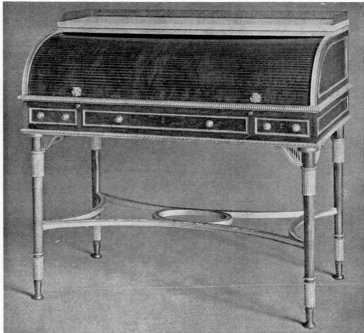

Fig. 4. Rosewood secretaire, with tambour front, brass gallery and ormolu mounts. c. 1800. Height, 3 ft 4 in.; length, 3 ft 5½ in.

Fig. 5. (*Above*) *Rosewood commode-chiffonier (one of a pair), mounted with ormolu. The design probably by Holland, c. 1800. Height (with bookcase), 4 ft 10½ in.; length, 5 ft 8 in.*

Fig. 6. (*Right*) *White marble chimney-piece, from the drawing-room, Southill, and chimney glass with carved and gilt frame and panel enriched with acanthus foliage relieved against a green ground (originally of velvet). c. 1800. Egyptian elements in the design of the chimney-piece (the female terminal figures in the niches) are derived probably from Tatham.*

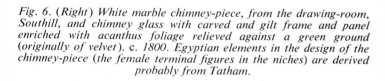

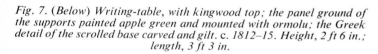

Fig. 7. (*Below*) *Writing-table, with kingwood top; the panel ground of the supports painted apple green and mounted with ormolu; the Greek detail of the scrolled base carved and gilt. c. 1812–15. Height, 2 ft 6 in.; length, 3 ft 3 in.*

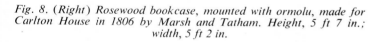

Fig. 8. (*Right*) *Rosewood bookcase, mounted with ormolu, made for Carlton House in 1806 by Marsh and Tatham. Height, 5 ft 7 in.; width, 5 ft 2 in.*

Fig. 9. (Above, left) Gilt armchair (one of a set), probably made by William Marsh to the design of Holland for the drawing-room at Southill, c. 1796–9, and rosewood footstool mounted with ormolu, c. 1807–10. Height (of chair), 2 ft 9¾ in.; height (of stool), 7 in.

Fig. 10. (Left) Gilt armchair (one of a set of four), in the 'Etruscan' style, made to the design of Holland for Sir William Lee at Colworth House, and later transferred to Hartwell (occupied from 1808–15 by the exiled Louis XVIII). c. 1796–9. See Fig. 9.

Fig. 11. (Above) Carved and gilt throne chair (one of a pair made by Tatham and Bailey at a cost of £587 12s. for Carlton House in 1813). Probably from a design by Charles Heathcote Tatham, based on drawings of Roman marble thrones. Height, 3 ft 6 in.; width, 3 ft.

cases were made by Marsh and Tatham, who in 1806 supplied several for Carlton House with 'rich ormolu mounts, ormolu ornaments, and plate glass and statuary ledges for the same'.[1]

In some furniture formerly at Hartwell[2] there is a close stylistic resemblance to some pieces at Southill, and they must be by the same maker (compare Figs. 9 and 10).

It is unfortunate that Holland died at the time when the revived classicism had established itself. In the year following his death furniture design was given a new direction by the *Household Furniture* of Thomas Hope (1807).

The successive stages of the Greek taste are recorded in publications which exhibit clearly the character of the revival, and the point at which it overweighs the sense of form and becomes antiquarian. A young artist, Moses, was encouraged by the success of Tatham's etchings of ancient ornament to bring out his less expensive collection of antique vases, altars,

paterae, tripods and candelabra in 1812. Richardson's *Collection of ornaments in the antique style* was published in 1816. Ackermann's *Ornaments for the Use of Sculptors, Painters and Modellers*, which was published in 1827, is based entirely on Greek detail. In a design for a pedestal by Richard Brown, in his *Rudiments of Drawing Cabinet and Upholstery Furniture* (1820), the brass ornament on the standard is taken from the cornice of the Parthenon, and another design stated to be 'the result of the author's study of Greek and Roman examples'. In 1822 it was said that the English 'is more chaste than the French Greek, and has advanced so rapidly during the last ten years that the French have adopted much of it'.[3]

[1] H. Clifford Smith, *Buckingham Palace* (1931), p. 23.

[2] These pieces were made for William Lee of Colworth, Member for Bedford, and friend of Samuel Whitbread of Southill.

[3] Cited in Architectural Publication Society's *Dictionary* (1842), under Furniture.

Fig. 12. *Richly carved and gilt settee (one of a set of four), supplied by Tatham and Bailey for Carlton House in 1810. Length, 6 ft 10 in.*

Fig. 13. *Mahogany wine cooler, with carved and gilt details. c. 1820. Height, 2 ft 2 in.; length, 3 ft 4 in.*

This idealisation of Greece was expressed by emphasising the elements of severity in furniture. As an archaeological reconstruction of Greek or Roman furniture was impossible, designers compromised, adapting the forms to serve the uses of the modern world. In France, Fontaine, who collaborated with Percier, wrote that they 'have followed the models of antiquity not blindly, but with discrimination entailed by the manners, customs and materials of the moderns'. Classical types of furniture were, however, closely followed, such as the couch, the cross-framed chair and stool, and the round table with lion feet.

Chairs, both in England and on the Continent, were by 1802 'of different shapes and patterns copied after the antique'. The bosses applied to the junction of the leg and seat rail in imitation of bolt heads suggest the influence of classical furniture.

The two gilt council chairs (Fig. 11) were supplied by Tatham and Bailey for Carlton House in 1813. The backs are solid to the ground and carved with Greek acanthus scrolls repeated on either side of a vertical line, and each of the front supports is composed of a winged sphinx. They resemble the marble thrones with solid sides and animal and sphinx supports of which Charles Heathcote Tatham published illustrations in his *Ancient Ornamental Architecture*[1] (compare Figs. 1 and 11).

The word 'Grecian' becomes part of the furniture-maker's vocabulary, and many of the sumptuous and costly pieces of furniture now in the state-rooms of Buckingham Palace, which

can be dated by the Royal accounts, are severely classic in form or detail, or in both. Examples of this classic furniture are the candelabra made by Tatham in 1811,[2] and the set of gilt settees made in 1810 by Tatham and Bailey for the crimson drawing-room at Carlton House (Fig. 12).

In architecture and furniture the aim was an extreme simplicity of form, with a partiality for large uninterrupted surfaces, unbroken lines and bold curves, and the reduction of ornament to a minor role.

The lion foot and lion monopodium and the lyre are also legacies from the classic antiquity. No detail was used more frequently than reeding, which emphasises structural lines, whether vertical or horizontal. The careful drawing of the acanthus leaves upon the wine-cooler (Fig. 13) and supports to the dining table from the Liverpool Town Hall is also characteristic of this revivalist furniture.

There is an increasing use of Greek *motifs* during the early nineteenth century. In Brown's *Rudiments* and in *The Practical Cabinet Maker, Upholsterer and Complete Decorator* (1826–7), by Peter and Michael Angelo Nicholson, much of the detail is of Greek origin, and a selection of ornaments from the safest and 'chastest' Greek sources is also supplied (Figs. 14 and 15).

[1] Such as the 'grand antique chair in Parian marble' in the Vatican Museum (Plate 84). In the Louvre is a marble seat supported by winged female sphinxes. Cf. Ransom, *Ancient Furniture*, Fig. 281.

[2] H. Clifford Smith, op. cit., Figs. 158 and 159.

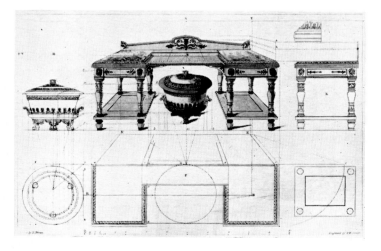

Fig. 14. *Design for a 'Tripod & Stand', from the Nicholsons'* Practical Cabinet Maker *(1826–1827), Plate 80.*

Fig. 15. *Design for a 'Sideboard', from Brown's* Rudiments *(2nd ed., 1822), Plate XIX.*

Furniture of Thomas Hope

THOMAS HOPE,[1] the banker and virtuoso, eldest of the sons of John Hope of Amsterdam, the descendant of a family of Amsterdam merchants, is an influential figure in the development of the classical revival and introduced severer forms in furniture. After a childhood spent in Holland, he came to London, where he had been preceded by other members of the Hope family, who had fled from their Dutch homes in fear of the French invasion of 1794.[2] As a young man he had had some architectural training, and prior to his arrival in England he had spent eight years in studying architectural remains in Greece, Turkey, Asia Minor, Syria and Egypt. Five volumes of his original drawings exist, containing a record of the antiquities of the Eastern Mediterranean at the close of the eighteenth century. His friendship with the French architect Percier brought him under the influence of a designer who, with his friend Fontaine, had given a definite classic form to the 'Empire' style; and his personal taste[3] inclined towards the rigidity of the new style. The interiors of Hope's London house in Duchess Street and of that at Deepdene in Surrey, designed as backgrounds for his collection of Egyptian and Roman sculptures, vases and objects of art, were an archaeological fantasy, the product of some learning and much enthusiasm. Whatever setting he chose, Greek, Roman or Egyptian, the scheme was carried out with consistent zeal.

Hope does not appear to have pushed his theories except by the issue of his *Household Furniture* (1807), for which he made most of the drawings. In it he writes that cabinet-makers had even before its publication directly imitated his furniture, that 'extravagant caricatures' had 'started up in every corner of the capital'. He pleads for 'that breadth and repose of surface . . .

that harmony and significance of accessories, and that apt accord between the peculiar meaning of each imitative or significant detail and the peculiar destination of the main object to which these accessories belonged, which are calculated to afford to the eye and mind the most lively, most permanent and most unfading enjoyment'.[4] It was a scholar's plea, and at home his system of significant detail was carried out. The London house was complete in 1804, when George Dance, who visited it, was of the opinion that 'by the singularity of it, good might be done, as it might contribute to emancipate the public taste from that rigid adherence to a certain style of architecture & of finishing, & unshackle the Artists'. The 'singularity' of the new classic movement lay in a close and archaeological reproduction of Roman furniture. In his *Household Furniture*, Hope illustrates a table of his design supported by 'chimaeras in bronze, similar to some limbs of ideal animals adapted to the same purpose, which have been found among the remains of Pompeii'. Preoccupied with this ideal severity, Hope aimed at making objects of modern use, a fire-screen, a bookcase and a side-board, congruous with the Roman tradition. In this he was successful; his new designs *were* congruous with the classic, and the ornamental detail consistently applied (Figs. 16 and 17). Hope's achievement can be studied in his *Household Furniture*,

[1] C. 1770–1831.
[2] H. W. and I. Law, *Book of the Beresford Hopes* (1925).
[3] He writes: 'I scarcely was able to hold a pencil when . . . I already began dealing with those straight lines which seem so little attractive to the general number' — *An Historical Essay on Architecture* (2nd ed., 1835), p. 183.
[4] P. 2.

Fig. 16. Design for a sofa, from Hope's Household Furniture *(1807), Plate 18, No. 5.*

Fig. 17. Design for a side-table, from Hope's Household Furniture *(1807), Plate 13, No. 3.*

Fig. 18. Mahogany bookcase, formerly at Deepdene, designed by Thomas Hope in the Egyptian taste. The Egyptian heads to the pilasters and the applied ornaments to the frieze and cupboards are in bronze of a dull green tint. c. 1810.

Fig. 19. Top of table (Fig. 20).

which is a record of the decoration and furniture at Duchess Street.[1] Examples of Hope's work are the bookcase in the Egyptian taste (Fig. 18), the table with its top inlaid with ebony and silver (Figs. 19 and 20) and the stands supported by lion monopodia (Fig. 21).

There is a marked change in the temper of criticism from the date of publication of his *Household Furniture* to the second decade of the nineteenth century. The book was at first ridiculed in the *Edinburgh Review*[2] as frivolous, and Dance's[3] reaction on seeing Hope's London house in 1804 was 'amusement'. The

reviewer's criticism of the weak points of Hope's design, such as its bulkiness, is to the point. It was 'too bulky, massive and ponderous to be commodious for general use', an 'assemblage of squared timber and massive brass as would weigh down the floor and crush out the walls of an ordinary London house'. But in the full tide of the Greek revival, his innovations were accepted as 'the beautifully classic change'.[4]

[1] Sculpture and furniture transferred at a later date from Duchess Street to Deepdene remained there practically undisturbed until 1917, when dispersed by auction.
[2] 1807, Vol. X, p. 478.   [3] *Farington Diary*, March 31, 1804.
[4] J. T. Smith, *Nollekens and His Times* (ed. Whitten, 1920). Vol. I, p. 175.

Fig. 20. Mahogany table, inlaid with ebony and silver, formerly at Deepdene. From a design by Thomas Hope, c. 1807. Height, 2 ft 4½ in.

Fig. 21. Mahogany tripod stand, supported by lion monopodia. From a design by Thomas Hope, based on Charles Heathcote Tatham's drawing of an antique tripod of Parian marble, first published in 1799. Formerly at Clumber. c. 1807. Height, 2 ft 9 in.; diameter of top, 1 ft 8 in.

Thomas Sheraton's *Cabinet Dictionary* and *Encyclopaedia* and George Smith's *Household Furniture*

THE earliest published designs for furniture in the Regency style are those contained in Sheraton's late works, the *Cabinet Dictionary* (1803) and the uncompleted *Encyclopaedia* (1804–6).[1] The designs are variable in quality and for the most part much inferior to those in the neo-classic style of the late eighteenth century that he had given some ten years earlier in the *Drawing Book*.[2] Sheraton's powers of invention were failing. He was a tired and sick man, who found it 'extremely difficult to attain to any thing really novel'.[3] It is doubtful if at that time he was able readily to accept the revolution of taste that had come about both in England and abroad, or to assimilate the new ideas that were current. Probably he had no access to such sources as Tatham's *Ancient Ornamental Architecture* (1799).[4] Formerly, he had made it his business 'to apply to the best workmen in different shops, to obtain their assistance in the explanation of such pieces as they have been most acquainted with'[5] and it is likely that the procedure was repeated in 1802–3 and that his impressions of the new style were based on close examination of finished work by fashionable London makers. He states that he had been 'favoured with a view' of the latest French chairs, which 'follow the antique taste, and introduce into their arms and legs, various heads of animals'.[6]

[1] *The Cabinet-Maker, Upholsterer and General Artist's Encyclopaedia* (issued in parts 1804–6).
[2] That the style persisted into the early years of the nineteenth century is evidenced by the publication of a third edition of the *Drawing Book* in 1802.
[3] *Cabinet Dictionary* (1803), p. 201.
[4] Reprinted in 1803, 1810 and 1836.
[5] *Drawing Book* (1791–4).
[6] *Cabinet Dictionary* (1803), p. 146.

The majority of Sheraton's *Cabinet Dictionary* and *Encyclopaedia* designs presumably were never executed. However, they were not without influence on production (Fig. 22). The designs incorporate various of the Regency forms and *motifs* that were to come into general use in the course of the next few years. He submits designs for the 'Grecian' chair, supported on incurving or swept legs of circular section (of a modified type, but figured in Ackermann's *Repository of Arts* as late as 1814), or on true 'sabre' legs; for chairs with cross-framed supports, based on the curule seat; for the 'Grecian' sofa with high back, and the couch with one low end; for tables with a central support springing from a platform with short splayed legs, or supported on end standards (Fig. 23). He introduces freely such *motifs* as the chimera monopodium, the lion or human mask, and the paw foot (Fig. 24). For a 'new design for a Pembroke table' (Fig. 25), as for certain other tables, he employs curved, cross-shaped end supports, decorated with reeding—an elegant form to become very fashionable during the early Regency, and one that was repeated in the 1820's (Figs. 26 and 27). He may have obtained his idea of it from French models (Fig. 28).

The picture provided by George Smith in *A Collection of Designs for Household Furniture and Interior Decoration* (1808) is more complete. Smith, in 1808, was a successful practising cabinet-maker, of, it may be estimated, some twenty years' experience. He was comparatively a young man, competent and ambitious (he declares himself as 'Upholder Extraordinary to His Royal Highness The Prince of Wales'). His *Household Furniture* is a comprehensive work, containing designs for a wide range of articles of furniture, in the various styles prevailing (Greek, Roman, Egyptian, Chinese and Gothic). There are

Fig. 22. Armchair (part of a set), with gilt enrichments; recalling a design by Sheraton in the Cabinet Dictionary *(1803), Plate 31. c. 1805.*

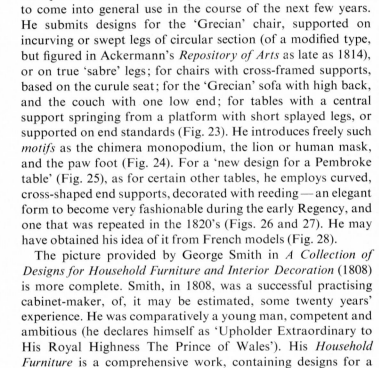

Fig. 23. Design for a sofa table, dated 1804, from Sheraton's Encyclopaedia *(1804–6), Plate 39.*

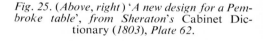

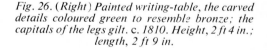

Fig. 24. Design for a 'Secretary & Bookcase', from Sheraton's Encyclopaedia *(1804–6), Plate 29.*

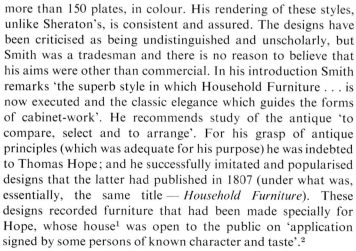

Fig. 25. (Above, right) 'A new design for a Pembroke table', from Sheraton's Cabinet Dictionary *(1803), Plate 62.*

Fig. 26. (Right) Painted writing-table, the carved details coloured green to resemble bronze; the capitals of the legs gilt. c. 1810. Height, 2 ft 4 in.; length, 2 ft 9 in.

more than 150 plates, in colour. His rendering of these styles, unlike Sheraton's, is consistent and assured. The designs have been criticised as being undistinguished and unscholarly, but Smith was a tradesman and there is no reason to believe that his aims were other than commercial. In his introduction Smith remarks 'the superb style in which Household Furniture . . . is now executed and the classic elegance which guides the forms of cabinet-work'. He recommends study of the antique 'to compare, select and to arrange'. For his grasp of antique principles (which was adequate for his purpose) he was indebted to Thomas Hope; and he successfully imitated and popularised designs that the latter had published in 1807 (under what was, essentially, the same title — *Household Furniture*). These designs recorded furniture that had been made specially for Hope, whose house[1] was open to the public on 'application signed by some persons of known character and taste'.[2]

Smith's designs for furniture are ornate and unimaginative. On the whole he favours rectilinear forms, avoiding curved

flowing lines. His furniture therefore is generally substantial in appearance, but lacks the elegance and liveliness that is often to be associated with Regency production (Fig. 29). A tendency to stiffness is to be seen in the designs for armchairs and other seat furniture (wherein he follows Hope). More often than not the arms are rigidly horizontal, meeting the supports (sometimes winged sphinxes) at right-angles. He makes considerable use of animal monopodia, singly or grouped, as supports for chairs, sideboards, tables and other articles. He popularised such *motifs* as the winged paw-foot and the columnar member with central lotus leaf ornament. The console end supports featured in certain designs for tables, library and hall seats, were again adapted directly from Hope, but derived via Tatham from the antique (Fig. 30).

[1] 'Mr Hope's house resembled a museum' — *Farington Diary*, October 23, 1812.
[2] C. M. Westmacott, *British Galleries of Painting and Sculpture* (1824).

Fig. 27. Design for a 'Ladies Toilette Table', from George Smith's Guide (1828), Plate XXVI.

Fig. 28. Writing-table, on a cross-membered frame of steel, with gilt bronze mounts. The top lifts up to disclose a fitted interior. The table bears the stamp of Weisweiler, Paris 1800. Height, 2 ft 6 in.; width, 2 ft 2½ in.

Fig. 29. Design for a 'Commode for Drawing Room', dated 1804, from George Smith's Household Furniture (1808), Plate 119.

Fig. 30. Design for a dressing-table, dated 1805, from George Smith's Household Furniture (1808), Plate 72. See Fig. 247.

The Egyptian Revival

THE attempt to naturalise Egyptian *motifs* and symbolism (and, in a few cases, architectural forms) dates from the first years of the nineteenth century. This revival follows upon Bonaparte's expedition to Syria and Egypt in 1798–1801, in which an archaeological mission duplicated Bonaparte's military staff, and a more intense interest was aroused in the art of Egypt, as surpassing in grandeur and strangeness any other of the visible works of man. After the campaign, Vivant Denon, the leading archaeologist of the expedition, had a bedroom fitted up by Jacob Desmalter to his own design in the Egyptian style. The bed, which was of mahogany inlaid with silver, had three sides ornamented with bas-reliefs of kneeling figures; its head was decorated with a carved Isis and the legs with the Uraeus.

Farington, who visited Paris in 1802, noticed in Napoleon's private apartment in the Tuileries that 'the Egyptian figure [of] the Sphynx made part of the frame work of the Chairs in one of the apartments',[1] and Egyptian detail is figured in Percier and Fontaine's *Recueil de Décorations Intérieures* (1812) and introduced in their decorations for Napoleon as first Consul.

Archaeologists and travellers, such as Volney and Grohmann,[2] had led the way in the exploration of Egypt during the late years of the eighteenth century, and Piranesi[3] had used Egyptian *motifs* in his designs, maintaining that what had been called its rigidity and harshness was only a sign of the 'harmonious force and solidity' of the style. To the influence of these early pioneers must be assigned the silver candelabrum and a pair of candlesticks bearing the London hallmarks for the

years 1791–2.[4] Egyptian *motifs* appear occasionally in Louis XVI furniture, and in the work of Henry Holland, who is known to have received drawings of Egyptian antiquities in Rome, made on his behalf between 1794 and 1796 by C. H. Tatham (Fig. 6).

It was, however, not until the publication of Denon's *Voyages dans la Basse et Haute Egypte* in 1802 that this archaeological revival had any large following in England.[5] Its publication 'gave use and life to a taste for this description of embellishment'[6] (Figs. 31 and 32). Its progress in this country (which also had its share in the Egyptian campaign) is recorded in magazines and architectural publications. In particular, Nelson's victory of the Nile (1798) had fostered a taste, which, by 1806, had affected 'many articles of interior decoration' and had become the 'present prevailing fashion'.[7] It was experimented in by Thomas Hope[8] (who had sketched the

---

[1] *Farington Diary*, September 11, 1802.

[2] Volney, *Voyage en Egypte* (1787). Translation of Norden's *Voyage d'Egypte et de Nubie* (1795). Grohmann, *Restes d'architecture Egyptienne* (1799).

[3] *Diverse maniere d'adornare i camini* (1769), Plate 14. The room, the *caffè inglese*, in the Piazza di Spagna, in Rome, must have been well known to travellers.

[4] Jackson, *Illustrated History of English Plate* (1911), Vol. II, p. 875.

[5] Holland possessed a copy of the work.

[6] George Smith, *Cabinet-Maker's and Upholsterer's Guide* (1828), p. vi. (Published in 1828, although engraved title page is dated 1826.)

[7] J. Randall, *A Collection of Architectural Designs for Mansions* (1806).

[8] In the bibliography in his *Household Furniture* Hope mentions Denon's and Norden's works as having been among the most useful to him.

Fig. 31. Rosewood table, with hinged section to the top and Egyptian supports, having heads and feet of brass. c. 1807.

Fig. 32. Pedestal library table, painted with figures and ornaments in the classic taste, and having the cupboards flanked by Egyptian terms. c. 1805. Length, 6 ft; depth, 4 ft.

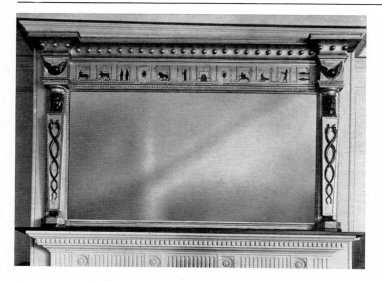

Fig. 33. Painted chimney mirror, decorated on the frieze with the signs of the Zodiac, and flanked by Egyptian terms. c. 1807. Height, 3 ft 1 in.

Fig. 34. Mahogany pedestal library table, made by Thomas Chippendale, the younger, in 1804–5 for Sir Richard Colt Hoare. ('A large mahogany Library table with pedestals and drawers inside pedestals, mahogany pannell'd doors, thermed legs with Philosophers' heads carved on Do. 4 end therms with Egyptian heads, the top part fitted up with drawers of fine wood, the whole made to take to pieces, and strong iron castors £115' — Thomas Chippendale's bill, 1805.) Height, 2 ft 6½ in.; length, 8 ft 3 in.

antiquities of Egypt for the room in which this part of his collections was housed). He was, of course, concerned with the more scholarly aspects of the taste. The decoration, designed to 'bear some analogy to its contents', was taken from Egyptian mummy cases and papyri, the colouring of the walls, ceiling and furniture pale yellow and bluish green, relieved by masses of black and gold. He was considered to have 'made a perfect hieroglyphic of most of our apartments'.[1] Hope warns the 'young artist' that this style is not to be lightly undertaken, 'the hieroglyphic figures, so universally employed by the Egyptians, can afford us little pleasure on account of their meaning since this is seldom intelligible'. A bookcase from Deepdene (Fig. 18), in his Egyptian manner, has the entablature supported by pilasters terminating in Egyptian heads, while the supports to the lower stage are lion-headed.

In spite of Hope's warning, Egyptian detail became the vogue (Fig. 33). At Crawley House, in Bedfordshire, the wall-paper of the drawing-room preserves its borders in which a mummy serves as a 'stop' to divide two sphinxes, and a chimney-glass in the same room is decorated with a lotus and anthemium frieze and 'Egyptian female heads to the pilasters', as entered in the upholsterer Collis's bill in 1806. At Harewood House, in Yorkshire, according to Jewell,[2] the entrance hall was 'fitted up in the Egyptian style', and in a description of White Knights, published in the same year, one room is described as 'ornamented with a painted cornice and capitals in the Egyptian manner', while the chimney-piece was 'sculptured in the same style of art, each side being supported by an Isis'.

At Stourhead in Wiltshire is a quantity of furniture in mahogany and satinwood made by the younger Thomas

[1] *Edinburgh Review* (1807), Vol. X, p. 485.
[2] Jewell, *Tourist's Companion* (1819), p. 21.

Chippendale for the Wiltshire antiquary, Sir Richard Colt Hoare, in the early years of the nineteenth century. Among the bills is an entry of a set of 'eight mahogany chairs with circular backs, broad sweep pannelled tops, with circle elbows, carved Egyptian heads and fluted therm feet, the rails moulded and carved, cane seats and brass socket castors' for the library, and the mahogany table and pedestal writing-table are also enriched with Egyptian, combined, in the case of the writing-table, with classic heads (Fig. 34). The tapering and fluted sheaths finish below in human feet, both in the engaged supports upon the front of the table and in the free-standing Egyptian supports between the plinth and semi-circular ends. The finely-finished heads are carved, not inserted in cast brass, which became customary in furniture of this type. Such decoration was often no more than superficial (Fig. 35).

A silver candelabrum in the style, which was made for the Duke of Cumberland in 1805, has the shaft in the form of a triform Egyptian figure resting on a triangular base supported by winged sphinxes. The candle branches are shaped as foliated scrolls terminating in dolphin heads (Fig. 36).

That the Egyptian style did not stop short at archaeological *motifs* we have the evidence of a description of a house in *Our Village*, in which the library is Egyptian, 'all covered with hieroglyphics and swarming with furniture crocodiles and Sphinxes'.[1] The sofa (Fig. 37), a piece of sheer extravagance which might have come from this library, is an unique survival of this swarm.

The Egyptian style was still approved by the Nicholsons as late as 1826, and may have lingered until about 1830.

[1] 'Only think of a crocodile couch and a Sphinx sofa' — Miss Mitford, *Our Village*, Vol. IV, pp. 239–40.

Fig. 36. Silver gilt candelabrum for seven lights, in the Egyptian taste. Made by Smith & Sharp for the Duke of Cumberland in 1805. Height, 3 ft.

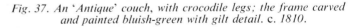

Fig. 37. An 'Antique' couch, with crocodile legs; the frame carved and painted bluish-green with gilt detail. c. 1810.

Fig. 35. Mahogany single chair, inlaid with ebonised lines. (The back panel was originally mounted with a crocodile in metal.) c. 1810.

The Chinese Taste

'EVEN the grotesque has its beauty' (so runs a passage in the English text of Piranesi's *Diverse maniere d'adornare i camini* of 1769),[1] and, therefore, though the Chinese taste was admittedly 'far distant from the Grecian and perhaps more so than the Egyptian and Tuscan, we are delighted to have our rooms and apartments fitted up after the Chinese manner'.

China, an object of curiosity intermittently through three centuries, was known by drawings in books of travel, and Sir William Chambers's *Designs for Chinese Buildings* (1757), du Halde's great work on the Chinese empire[2] and the embassy of Lord Macartney in 1792–4 had enlightened and clarified English taste. The attraction of Chinese art was readily comprehensible. It was an art of exquisite finish (but not to the European eye consistent), and it was an escape from the discipline of the five orders.

Interest in Chinese art, which was revived just before the middle of the eighteenth century, continued in a crescendo of fashionable whim and caprice until the classical revival under Robert Adam. The style thus established as a fashion was constantly ridiculed in the mid-eighteenth century, and in a discussion of its merits by Alison in his *Essays on Taste*, the admiration of the 'fantastic and uncouth' forms of this Anglo-Oriental art is explained as due to association. 'They were universally admired because they brought to mind those images of Eastern magnificence and splendour of which we have heard so much, and which we are always willing to believe because they are distant'[3] — an example of the romantic fallacy which idealises the distant, both in time and place, and identifies beauty with the unfamiliar.[4]

The last revival during the Regency owes something to the personal taste of George IV when Prince of Wales. When alterations were being made in the Brighton Pavilion in 1802, 'several pieces of very beautiful Chinese paper were presented to the Prince, who for a time was undecided in what way to make use of them. Finally they were hung in a Chinese gallery, and the other parts of the gallery painted and decorated in a corresponding style.'[5]

Much of the interior of the Pavilion, with its palm tree columns, and 'the fantastic forms that raise themselves with the bravest fanfares of rhetoric',[6] witnesses to the Prince of Wales's experiments in this novel version of the Chinese taste (Fig. 38).

That the Chinese taste had already engaged the attention of the Prince of Wales before that date there is the evidence of his

[1] P. 10.
[2] J. B. du Halde, *Description de l'Empire de la Chine* (1735).
[3] Archibald Alison, *Essays on Taste* (ed. 1815), p. 195.
[4] See Geoffrey Scott, *The Architecture of Humanism*, p. 39.
[5] E. W. Brayley, *Illustrations of Her Majesty's Palace at Brighton* (1838).
[6] Osbert Sitwell, *The Scarlet Tree* (1946), p. 7.

Fig. 38. Shelved cabinet, with framework in imitation of bamboo; the cupboard doors, enclosing two tiers of shallow drawers, japanned in the Chinese taste in black and gold; the winged claw feet gilt. Made for the Royal Pavilion, Brighton. c. 1808. Height, 3ft 1½ in.; length, 7 ft 10 in.

I. The King's Bedroom, The Royal Pavilion, Brighton.

Chinese drawing-room at Carlton House, described and illustrated by Sheraton in the *Drawing Book*. The walls of the room were divided by 'Chinese columns' and the panels painted with 'Chinese views and little scenes'. Among its contents were two pairs of side- or pier-tables of ebony veneered on oak, with ormolu mounts and tops of red marble (Figs. 39 and 40). These were of French origin, made probably by Adam Weisweiler about 1782. (Through Henry Holland, a considerable amount of fine Louis XVI furniture had been purchased for Carlton House in the closing years of the eighteenth century.) The tables were brought to the Pavilion [together with Chinese export furniture of bamboo (Fig. 41)] in 1802, when the work of creating a Chinese interior was begun. The taste for 'Chinese' furniture was carried on for the decoration of the Brighton Pavilion when it took its final form from 1815 to 1822, and was chiefly executed by the firm of Crace and Robert Jones. Among furniture designed by Robert Jones, and made by Bailey & Saunders, are side-tables of rosewood supported by carved dragons supplied in 1817 for the Banqueting room.

This furniture in the Chinese taste was, like that of the eighteenth-century revival, marked by angularity, by a predilection for gay and tortuous forms, and for Chinese *motifs* such as the dragon and the pagoda, and by the introduction of Chinese figures (Figs. 42 and 43). In the framework of chairs and light tables bamboo was frequently simulated; the surface of furniture was japanned and decorated in imitation of Chinese lacquer (Plate I), and there are instances of the use of pseudo-Chinese inscriptions (Fig. 44). Panels of true Oriental lacquer, both Chinese and Japanese, were made use of by English makers for such articles as commodes and cabinets (Fig. 45).

Fig. 40. Detail of Fig. 39. The drapery, hanging from a 'bamboo' rod, and the surmounting dragon are of ormolu.

Fig. 41. (Right) Bamboo caned chair, made in China for the European market. Originally used in the saloon of the Royal Pavilion, Brighton. c. 1800. Height, 3 ft; width, 1 ft 7 in.; depth, 1 ft 5 in.

Fig. 42. Single chair, japanned in black and gold. c. 1815. See Fig. 43. Height, 2 ft 9½ in.; width, 1 ft 6 in.

Fig. 43. Sofa of beech, japanned black, and decorated with gilt detail. c. 1815. See Fig. 42. Height, 2 ft 11 in.; length, 6 ft 8½ in.

Fig. 44. Commode, inlaid with ebonised lines and mounted with panels of lacquer and pseudo-Chinese inscriptions. c. 1800. Height, 3 ft 3¾ in.; length, 4 ft 3¼ in.

Fig. 45. Commode, decorated with Japanese lacquer in gold on a black ground, with carved and gilt wood balusters and feet. c. 1815. Height, 2 ft 2½ in.; length, 3 ft 6¼ in.

The Gothic Taste

THE revived Gothic taste appears to date from the first decade of the new century: designs for Gothic furniture are included both in Sheraton's last work, the uncompleted *Encyclopaedia* (1804–6) and, more importantly, in George Smith's *Household Furniture* (1808).

Sheraton, before his death, was of unsound mind, and the pages of the *Encyclopaedia* bear witness to his mental deterioration; nevertheless, the designs provide a reliable indication of trends of fashion in the trade. Sheraton was 'bred to the cabinet business' and understood it, and he was perceptive of change.

Smith's designs are, he claims, studied from the best antique sources, some 'after the Gothic, or Old English fashion'. Gothic, we are told, admits 'of a more abundant variety of ornaments and forms than can possibly be obtained in any other style'. In fact, he offers numerous Gothic designs — for drawing-room, parlour and hall chairs; for drawing-room decoration, for a sofa table, quartetto tables, and canterburys;

for bedroom and for library furniture (for which the Gothic style was so generally approved) (Figs. 46 and 47). They are, on the whole, intended for execution in oak — the 'correct' wood and one offering practical advantages to the carver. A particularly elaborate design for a Gothic state bed is deemed not unacceptable, 'as many mansions of our Nobility and Gentry are at this time finished in a similar taste' (Fig. 48). Smith's designs in this style have a certain liveliness and interest; they are, at least, characteristic of their period, despite the attempt made to reproduce various Gothic forms and detail (Fig. 49).[1] In practice, the Gothic elements are often almost entirely subordinated to early nineteenth-century requirements

[1] ' "Regency" connotes less a specific style than a characteristic flavour given to a variety of styles — Gothic, Indian, Egyptian, or "Old English" as often as Roman or Greek — by the eclectic scholarship of the age' — Christopher Hussey, *English Country Houses: Late Georgian 1800–1840* (1958), p. 13.

Fig. 46. Design for a 'Library Bookcase', dated 1807, from George Smith's Household Furniture *(1808), Plate 103.*

Fig. 47. Mahogany break-front bookcase, in the Gothic taste, in the style of George Smith. c. 1808. See Fig. 46. Height, 9 ft; width, 7 ft 10½ in.

Fig. 48. From J. C. Buckler's Views of Eaton Hall in Cheshire (1826)
— the Drawing Room.

Fig. 49. (Right) Design for a lady's dressing-table and glass, dated
1807, from George Smith's Household Furniture (1808), Plate 74.

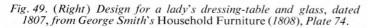

Fig. 50. Olivewood bookcase, fitted with secretaire drawer, and ornamented
with brass inlays; the glazed doors of the upper stage of 'Gothic' character.
c. 1800. Width, 3 ft 10 in.

Fig. 51. Library bookcase of mahogany, veneered with rosewood
(one of a pair made apparently as wall fixtures), in the Gothic taste.
The cluster columns which frame upper and lower parts are ringed
with brass. The bookcase is supported on a platform base. c. 1830.
Height, 7 ft 6 in.; width, 3 ft 9 in.; depth, 1 ft 6 in.

(Figs. 50–52). Regency Gothic or 'Old English' furniture was most appropriately placed in the *cottages ornées*, the new Gothic villas and mansions (Fig. 53).

There was probably small demand for furniture in the 'true Gothic style' during the first quarter of the century. Such furniture was appreciably more expensive than that in 'the modern style', and its execution required skills not possessed by the average workman, although simple furniture 'composed after designs which prevailed in the sixteenth century'[1] enjoyed some popularity. 'What passes for Gothic furniture among cabinet-makers and upholsterers', states Loudon in 1833, 'is, generally, a very different thing from the correct Gothic designs supplied by Architects who have imbued their minds with this style of art.'[2]

From 1825, however, a series of Gothic designs, antiquarian in character and incorporating with some accuracy fourteenth- and fifteenth-century ornament, was issued in Ackermann's *Repository of Arts*. The Gothic style, 'shown to be so well adapted to domestic arrangements and decorations', was then reported as 'becoming much more general'[3] (Fig. 54). These designs (by the elder Pugin) were published separately in 1829 under the title *Gothic Furniture*.[4] In this work the didactic approach of early Victorian designers towards Gothic is fore-shadowed.

[1] Ackermann's *Repository of Arts*, July 1813.
[2] *Encyclopaedia of Cottage, Farm, and Villa Architecture and Furniture* (ed. 1835), p. 1088.
[3] October, 1827.   [4] Augustus Charles Pugin (1762–1832).

Fig. 52. (Above) Dwarf cupboard, with superstructure of shelves painted cream and decorated with flowers and leaves in shades of green. The 'Gothic' detail introduced at the top is incidental and does not affect the form of the piece. c. 1815–20.

Fig. 53. (Above, right) Design for a cottage ornée, from J. B. Papworth's Rural Residences (1818), Plate 6.

Fig. 54. (Right) Gilt armchair (one of a pair), in the Gothic taste, upholstered in contemporary brown velvet, with silk embroidery. c. 1825–30.

The French Taste

IN the early 1790's a considerable amount of Louis XVI furniture had been brought into England by French *émigrés*. Much of this furniture (in the neo-classic style, developed under the *Directoire* and the *Empire*) was sold on the London market. A number of French craftsmen who had fled the Revolution, also settled and worked in this country. French influence is reflected in furniture supplied for Carlton House under Holland's direction, and in many of Sheraton's designs for the *Drawing Book* (1791–4).

Sheraton, however, in the *Cabinet Dictionary* (1803) condemns 'stupidly absurd prejudices' that then prevailed. 'A clumsy three-footed stool from France', he says, 'will be admired by our connoisseurs, in preference to a first rate cabinet of English production. We poor Englishmen are hardly able to judge of the due projection of a torus, of the beauty of a simple curve, nor even of a right line, except we borrow these from a French plan!'[1]

The direction given to French taste during the Consulate period was approved by Hope; he was by nature sympathetic to the austerities of the style. He was personally acquainted with both Percier and Fontaine, and expresses in *Household Furniture* his indebtedness to the former's *Edifices de Rome Moderne* — as also to such sources as Denon's *Voyages dans la Basse et Haute Egypte* (1802) and Le Roy's *Monuments de la Grèce*.

In 1812 (the year of publication of Percier and Fontaine's *Recueil*), Ackermann's *Repository of Arts* issued in successive numbers various designs for furniture in the style of the French Empire. And designs of this character appeared again in February 1815, when it is stated that the 'interchange of feeling between this country and France, as it relates to matters of taste, has not been wholly suspended during the long and awful conflicts which have so greatly abridged the intercourse of the two nations, and as usual the taste of both has been improved'. In 1822 it is reported that 'the taste for French furniture is carried to such an extent, that most elegantly furnished mansions, particularly in the sleeping rooms, are fitted up in the French style'. Certain London cabinet-makers[2] appear at this time to have specialised in the production of furniture of purely French character. Certainly French models were often closely copied.

The vogue for Boulle marquetry furniture, which obtained in France throughout the eighteenth century[3] and persisted after the Revolution, had spread to England on the lead given by the Prince Regent. Its popularity is evidenced by the setting up,

[1] P. 116.
[2] For example, William Snell of Albemarle Street (see 'Records of Furniture Makers').
[3] In 1772, Mariette (*Abecedario*) states: '*Les meubles de Boulle d'un goût exquis sont plus recherchés que jamais*'.

Fig. 55. Circular table of finely figured rosewood, elaborately decorated with brass marquetry of cursive character; supported on a massive concave-sided pedestal, resting on stylised paw feet. The top of the table and sides of the pedestal are edged with beading. c. 1815–20. See Fig. 20, the prototype table designed by Hope. Diameter of top, 4 ft; height, 2 ft 4½ in.

from about 1815, of 'English Buhl Manufactories', as those opened by Louis Le Gaigneur in Queen Street, Edgware Road, and Thomas Parker in Air Street. From about this time too an elaborate brass inlay or marquetry ornament, inspired by Boulle furniture, was commonly employed for many pieces of standard pattern[1] (Figs. 55–7, 66–7). Oakley's, as early as 1810, had supplied the Prince Regent with 'a capital mahogany pedestal library-table inlaid with Buhl bordering'.

The revived Louis XIV style, which emerged in France under the reigns of Louis XVIII (1815–24) and Charles X (1824–30), was adopted also to some extent in England. Smith's *Guide* (1828) contains a design for a 'Louis Quatorze' room (based apparently on the interior of Crockford's gaming house, Piccadilly, which had been remodelled by the Wyatt brothers). A contributor to the *Repository of Arts*, in 1828, refers disparagingly, however, to 'the heavy, cumbrous, and . . . unmeaning decoration of the style denominated that of Louis XIV'. Loudon, in 1833, describes it as 'characterised by curved lines and excess of curvilinear ornaments', and as 'unsuitable to the present advancing state of the public taste'. Much furniture, he states, 'formerly almost exclusively used by the great, has been exposed for sale, and consequently has attracted the notice of gentlemen of less opulence; and this has called into exercise a taste among them which had lain dormant for many years'. The change had come about 'in consequence of the first French revolution'.

[1] See 'Materials and Processes', pp. 44–5.

Fig. 56. (Above, right) Rosewood cabinet, or commode-chiffonier, with shelved superstructure fitted with a brass gallery; decorated with brass marquetry and metal enrichments. In the style of Louis Le Gaigneur, c. 1815. Height, 4 ft 10 in.; width, 3 ft 3 in.

Fig. 57. (Right) Rosewood circular table, with top of inlaid marble, supported on a central pillar with triangular platform base; the winged paw feet carved and gilt; the frieze and base decorated with brass marquetry. c. 1820. Height, 2 ft 5 in.; diameter of top, 2 ft 5½ in.

The Later Regency

THE Regency style came to maturity during the second decade of the century — appropriately, the years of the constitutional Regency (1811–20). Various models, forms and *motifs*, lately introduced, had been absorbed by the trade in general and were passing into common production.[1] Cabinet-makers, although reluctant to abandon established types of furniture and constructions, and conservative usually in their approach to change, were anxious to exploit fashion, if only by making use of selected features. 'Regency' has been called a '*mélange* or mixture of all styles' — Greek, Roman, 'Etruscan', Egyptian, Chinese and Gothic. The movement, however, despite the eclecticism of Regency taste, was predominantly archaeological. The publication of a third English edition of Tatham's *Ancient Ornamental Architecture* in 1810 and of George Smith's *A Collection of Ornamental Designs after the Manner of the Antique* (1812) suggests that interest in the 'Greek' as interpreted by Tatham and Hope still prevailed. Smith appears to have been indebted to Tatham for much of his material and refers to the 'generally diffused knowledge of the classic designs of Grecian workmanship'. His designs were intended for the use of 'Every Trade dependent on the Fine Arts'.

In 1815, the French war was brought to a successful conclusion;[2] thereafter the mood of the country was exultant, and fashion at its most ostentatious. Furniture was often of massive proportions and substance. There was a growing tendency for woods of lighter colour (amboyna and kingwood), and native woods such as pollarded elm, to supersede mahogany and rosewood; satinwood returned to favour. Ornament was more profusely employed, and naturalistic in character. Scrolling leaf and flower forms were preferred to the formal classical *motifs* of earlier years.

Richard Brown comments with some degree of satisfaction on the style prevailing in 1820. 'Before the cabinet-makers were acquainted with the works of the Greek school, and had acquired a knowledge of drawing', he writes, 'their designs were made up of the most trivial conceits . . . their furniture was consequently quite void of taste . . . and labour was wasted upon transient whims or puerile fashion. But within these few years, their productions have assumed a new character, bold in the outline, rich and chaste in the ornaments, and durable from the rejection of little parts. This style . . . has evidently arisen in a great measure from Mr Hope's mythological work on Household Furniture, Mr Smith's excellent book of Unique Designs, and Percier's splendid French work on Interior Decoration.'[3] . . .

Brown's *Rudiments* was the first of several pattern books to appear illustrating the character of the last phase of Regency taste. The designs, although few in number, are distinctive; their 'new character' is in large part due to Brown's use of heavy turned members (Figs. 15, 58 and 59). The *Rudiments* was followed in the later 1820's by John Taylor's *Upholsterer's and Cabinet Maker's Pocket Assistant* (c. 1825), Henry Whitaker's *Designs of Cabinet and Upholstery Furniture in the Most Modern Style* (1825), the Nicholsons' *Practical Cabinet Maker* (1826–7) and George Smith's last work, the *Guide* (1828) (Figs. 14, 27, 60–4 and 163). Of these, the most individual and accomplished is the *Practical Cabinet Maker*. Peter Nicholson, a Scottish architect and mathematician of some reputation who had set up in practice at Glasgow in 1800, was the leading spirit in the publication; his son, Michael Angelo, an architectural draughtsman and an occasional exhibitor at the Royal Academy, was responsible for the plates. Peter Nicholson was an energetic and versatile man and in youth had had practical experience of the cabinet trade. He had published numerous books of a technical nature. He had been concerned in promoting education among artisans, and his aim in undertaking the *Practical Cabinet Maker* was doubtless in large part corrective. The Nicholsons' designs, mainly in the 'Grecian' taste, are well conceived and exhibit a consistent style, and the book sets a standard against which competing works may be measured. It was published with the approbation of certain leading London cabinet-makers,[4] and commended 'to the notice of the trade'. Its influence on contemporary taste was beneficial and probably substantial. Taylor's designs for furniture and drapery were issued without text in two small volumes. The author, at one time employed as a designer by Oakley's, 'the most tasteful of London's cabinet-makers', was at the date of publication in business as an upholsterer in the neighbourhood of Covent Garden, and his patterns, therefore, may be thought to reflect current fashions. His 'pocket guide' illustrates articles for which

---

[1] In 1812, a number of Sheraton's late designs, which had appeared in the *Cabinet Dictionary* (1803) and in the *Encyclopaedia* (1804–6), were reissued posthumously as *Designs for Household Furniture* (the title echoing those adopted by Hope and Smith). This work contained patterns 'in the Cabinet, Chair, and Upholstery Branches on Eighty-four plates'.

[2] 'The average standard of life was almost certainly higher than in the previous century, if all regions and all classes are taken into account' — G. M. Trevelyan, *English Social History* (ed. 1946), p. 472.

[3] *Rudiments* (1820).

[4] Including Thomas and George Seddon, Aldersgate Street; Edward Bailey 'Manufacturer to His Majesty', Mount Street; and John Bywater, 'Upholsterer to His Majesty', Grosvenor Street.

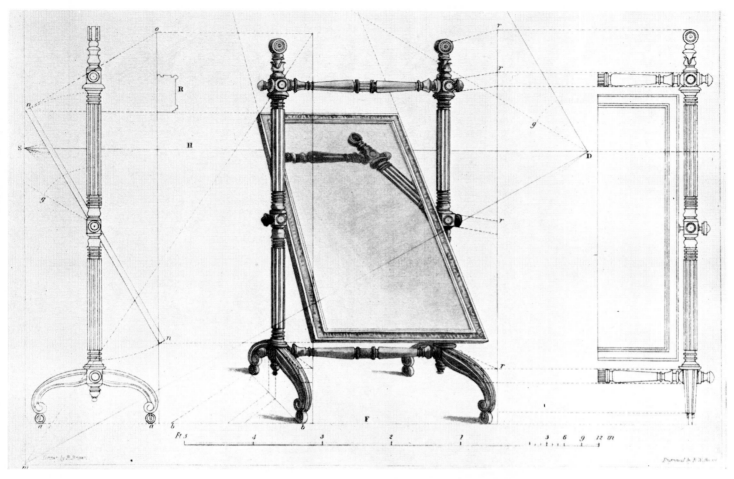

Fig. 58. Design for a 'Cheval Looking Glass', from Brown's Rudiments
(2nd ed., 1822), Plate XVI.

Fig. 59. Design for a 'Lady's Book-Case, with Cabinet', from Brown's
Rudiments *(2nd ed., 1822), Plate XVIII. The ornament, lavishly
employed as decoration for flat surfaces, is naturalistic in form. The
supports of the lower stage of the piece are disengaged.*

Fig. 60. Design for a pedestal sideboard, from Taylor's Upholsterer's
and Cabinet Maker's Pocket Assistant (c. 1825), *Vol. 2, Plate 3. The
heavy foliate cresting (of the back-board) is a prominent feature and
characteristic of fashionable taste in the 1820's. See also Fig. 61.*

some demand existed. The designs (many in the French style) are undistinguished and, stylistically, of mixed character, the more advanced embodying new features that were becoming current in the trade, such as heavily turned and grossly formed peg-top feet for tables and cabinets; brackets and colonnettes with brass mounts are much in evidence.

Smith's designs for the *Guide* (most of which date from 1826) have the merit of breaking new ground. In his preface, he recalls that he has had an experience of forty years of the furnishing trade, both in theory and practice. He appears to have accepted the fact that the Regency style was in the process of disintegration, and makes no attempt to prolong the period of its active life by developing ideas to which he had first given expression in his *Household Furniture* of 1808. This work is dismissed as having become 'wholly obsolete and inapplicable to its intended purpose, by the change of taste and rapid improvements' of past years. The *Guide* is a lengthy and ambitious work, with numerous coloured plates. Smith's tone is complacent, and the text pretentious; he includes various treatises on geometry, perspective and ornament, and offers an 'Historical View of the Origin of the Art in this Country'.

The 'change of taste', to which Smith refers, is described by Loudon — in a work which differs considerably from those of the foregoing authors (whose published designs for furniture, intended for execution, exerted a formative influence on style, at least in the case of Brown and the Nicholsons). Loudon's *Encyclopaedia* (*An Encyclopaedia of Cottage, Farm, and Villa Architecture and Furniture; containing numerous designs for dwellings, from the cottage to the villa ... with the requisite fittings-up, fixtures, and furniture*) was first published in 1833, reprinted in 1835 and in later editions (Fig. 65). Loudon, who was appreciative of the changing condition of society and optimistic of progress, aimed at 'rendering general a knowledge of Domestic Architecture' and 'increasing the comforts of the great mass of society'. His objective was to show how all dwellings might 'be equalized in point of all essential comforts, conveniences, and beauties'. He reported on the furniture that was available for different classes and commented on its suitability. The *Encyclopaedia* is illustrated by more than two thousand small engravings, of which a fair proportion are of articles of furniture.

'In giving Designs for the Furniture of Villas', he admits the

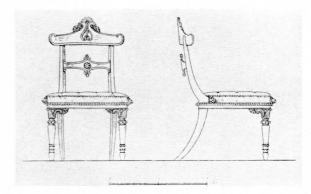

Fig. 61. *Design for a single chair, from Whitaker's* Cabinet and Upholstery Furniture (*1825*), *Plate 18.*

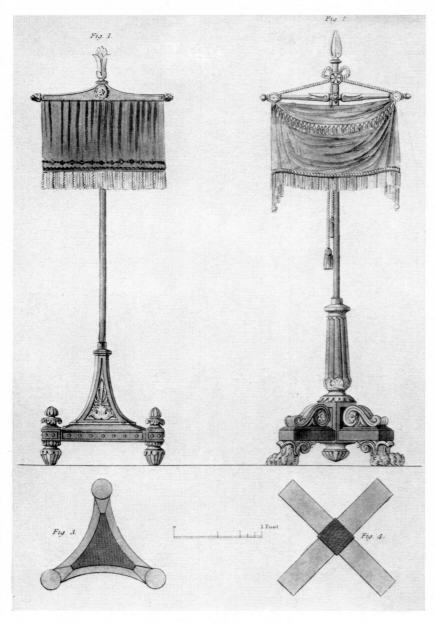

Fig. 62. *Design for 'Two Fire Screens', from the Nicholsons'* Practical Cabinet Maker (*1826–7*), *Plate 54.*

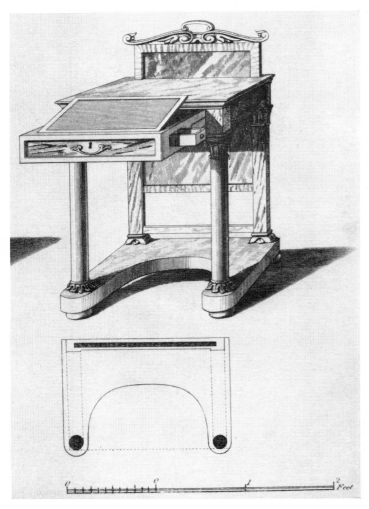

Fig. 63. Design for a 'Ladies Screen Writing Table', from George Smith's Guide (1828), Plate LXXXIII.

Fig. 64. (Below, left) Design for a 'Bookcase for a Study', dated 1826, from George Smith's Guide (1828), Plate XLI.

Fig. 65. (Above) Designs for furniture, from Loudon's Encyclopaedia (2nd ed., 1835): 'Two different patterns of chess tables, richly ornamented, and considered handsome'; a sideboard 'in what Architects call cabinet-maker's Gothic . . . neat and plain, but [having] no claim to merit in point of style'; and a pedestal sideboard with 'open sarcophagus-shaped wine-cooler beneath'.

existence of four principal styles: 'the Grecian or modern style . . . , the Gothic or perpendicular style, which imitates the lines and angles of the Tudor Gothic Architecture; the Elizabethan style, which combines the Gothic with the Roman or Italian manner; and the style of the age of Louis XIV, or the florid Italian'. Loudon's main classification is 'Grecian and Modern Furniture' — which is 'by far the most general'. But the designs illustrated in this section ('almost entirely made by Mr. Dalziel' and representative of articles 'executed in his manufactory'),[1] far from being in the 'pure Grecian taste' often incorporate elements borrowed from the so-called 'Gothic', 'Elizabethan' and 'Louis XIV' styles. They have little merit and illustrate the hybrid and uncertain nature of pre-Victorian taste. They are, as is observed of certain chairs that are illustrated, 'much more like the efforts of a mechanic in search of novelty' than of an architect or other artist. Dalziel's patterns for furniture often recall those of the 1820's, but the forms employed (overshadowed by the impending neo-rococo style of the mid-century) are swollen and weakened, and the ornament is coarse.

By 1833, creative design was clearly at a depressed level. 'The essential cause' was 'want of discrimination on the part of the public'. There existed, in London, an enormous demand for cabinet furniture by a large and newly prosperous middle class. 'So ardent' was 'the desire for novelty that the great and incessant efforts of the upholsterer' were directed towards its satisfaction. But 'instead of being met by taste and invention' the demand, he says, had called forth only 'mechanical changes or combinations of forms'. There was a marked deficiency of 'what is really original design in composition'.[2,3]

Furniture on the whole was well constructed, but largely 'mass-produced' and 'made in the piece'. Ordinary articles, such as the various sofa tables figured in the *Encyclopaedia*, 'both the good and the bad', were 'made in hundreds by the London cabinet-makers', for an enlarging public. According to Loudon, people wanted 'a display of rich workmanship, at as cheap a rate as possible', and taste was of 'a vulgar and grovelling kind'.[4] 'Cabinet Warehouses' selling 'ready-made furniture', or retail shops (of a type that had emerged in the later eighteenth century), were on the increase, and their proprietors were usually middlemen, not master cabinet-makers. New and improved methods of manufacture[5] contributed also towards the process of standardisation of types of furniture, and of ornament.

[1] William Dalziel, upholsterer and cabinet-maker, of 24 Great James Street, Bedford Row.

[2] *Encyclopaedia* (ed. 1835), pp. 1039, 1063, 1083.

[3] This much is suggested, indirectly, in the following passage, wherein Loudon, commenting on the 'Elizabethan' style, observes: 'it is seldom necessary to manufacture objects in this manner, farther than by putting together ancient fragments . . . we now have upholsterers in London who collect, both in foreign countries and in England, whatever they can find of ancient and curious furniture . . . and rearrange these curious specimens, and adapt them to modern uses'. He names Wilkinson and Wornum, of 315 Oxford Street, and James Nixon, of 123 Great Portland Street — p. 1039.

[4] Pp. 1068, 1041.

[5] The development of lathes meant that straight members were readily ornamented by turning at a very cheap rate; turned work became coarsened and over-elaborated, and deep cutting was the rule.

Materials and Processes

THE economic conditions resulting from the French war, which 'doubled the cost and trebled the difficulty of genteel living', made it desirable for furniture to be plainer and less costly; in the form of furniture, and in its technique, there were revolutionary changes. The curvature of fine furniture of the late eighteenth century meant expensive production, and, in general, in Regency furniture, surfaces (except in the case of some animal legs of classic type) were straight. The difficult years of the Napoleonic Wars[1] probably caused the disappearance of inlaying (*i.e.* wood marquetry) which Sheraton, in his *Cabinet Dictionary*, terms a 'very expensive mode of ornamenting furniture, as well as being subject to a speedy decay'.[2]

The craft of the carver in wood declined rapidly in the early nineteenth century, when there were only eleven master carvers in London, and about sixty journeymen. Many of the latter, we are told, 'are now very old; they make no shew of their work' and 'carving in wood has long been in the background as a branch of the arts'.[3, 4] Carving was sparingly employed, and was often bronzed or gilt, a sign of the dominance of metal technique.

WOODS

Greater stress, therefore, was laid upon the employment of dark lustrous cabinet woods, such as mahogany (which

[1] 'These costly times when Labour and materials . . . are so extravagantly dear' — D. Laing, *Hints for Dwellings* (1801), p. vii.

[2] P. 257.

[3] T. Martin, *The Circle of the Mechanical Arts* (1813), p. 211.

[4] An oblong panel of pearwood, dated 1807, in the corridor ante-chamber at Windsor Castle, is evidence of the skill of the unknown craftsman, who rivals Grinling Gibbons in the dexterity of his technique. It is executed entirely from one piece of pearwood, 'cut and undercut to the greatest depth and elaboration' — Sir G. Laking, *The Furniture of Windsor Castle* (1905), p. 58.

Fig. 66. Sofa table of amboyna (one of three) inlaid with brass, made in 1816 for Claremont (Esher, Surrey) for Princess Charlotte. Height, 2 ft 4¼ in.; length (extended), 4 ft 9 in.

Fig. 67. Grand piano of walnut, elaborately decorated with brass marquetry and inlay, supported on a triangular pedestal with concave sides. Inscribed above the keyboard: 'Patent Sostenente Grand, By I. H. R. Mott, C. Mott and Comp., 95, Pall Mall, London. Makers to His Majesty.' (Isaac, Henry and Robert Mott's patent was taken out in 1817). Made for the Prince Regent for the Music Room at the Royal Pavilion, Brighton, about 1818. Height, 3 ft; length, 8 ft 1 in.; width, 3 ft 11 in.

remained in general use, particularly for library furniture) and kingwood, and woods of marked figure, such as calamander wood, zebrawood and amboyna.

In 'dressed apartments' East and West Indian satinwood was used, as well as rosewood and 'other varieties of woods brought from the East',[1] but the strong lemon colour of satinwood was relieved not by marquetry, but by inlay of ebony[2] (or sometimes rosewood), with striking effect.

'Rosewood', a trade term which includes several species of wood (*Dalbergia nigra* and *Dalbergia latifolia*), is heavy, dense, and has dark streaks. The great vogue for rosewood was to some extent due to the opening of a direct trade with Spanish America and the Portuguese territories of South America during the Napoleonic wars. Brazil, from which rosewood was imported, was one of the most important of these new markets.

The wood known to cabinet-makers as kingwood, and highly prized by them from the late seventeenth century, is the produce of some varieties of trees from South America, having timber of 'a rich violet grain, shading sometimes almost to black, and streaked with varying lighter and darker markings of golden yellow'.[3] It has a bright lustre, and a very smooth surface, and is finer in the grain than rosewood.

Amboyna is a name given to burr wood imported from the Moluccas (including Amboyna) and Borneo. The wood is brown in colour, tinged with yellow or reddish-yellow, and is 'marked with little twisted curls and knots in a manner similar to, but more varied than, birds'-eye maple'.[4]

These woods were used largely as veneers. Regency furniture, if not intended for gilding, painting or japanning, was commonly veneered work. (Chairs and often dining tables provide an exception.) Veneer-cut woods exhibit great variety and richness of figure; it was, moreover, to the advantage of cabinet-makers to economise in the use of scarce and expensive timber. A considerable use was made, too, of veneers with a striped or marbled figure for cabinets and small tables. Among these was calamander wood, imported from India and Ceylon, which shows bands and streaks of black and brown.[5] It is described as yielding veneers of unusual beauty, dark wavings and blotches, almost black, being gracefully disposed over a delicate fawn-coloured ground. Zebrawood, 'streaked with brown and white as the animal is, whence it had the name',[6] has a similar effective figure, and firm hard texture, capable of a high polish, and was imported from Brazil. It was noticed as early as 1803 that supplies of this wood were scarce, and by

[1] George Smith, *Household Furniture* (1808), p. xiv.

[2] Bill of Samuel Beckwith — 'Two sattinwood shiffoniers ornamented with black lines inlaid'. For the drawing-room, Windsor Castle. Tradesmen's accounts, Lord Chamberlain's Office.

[3] Howard, *Manual of Timbers of the World* (ed. 1934), p. 247.

[4] The second Duke of Northumberland (d. 1817) was sent by the King of Portugal some 'unsawed timber called amboyna wood', and from this were made tables, chairs and settees, formerly in the ante-drawing-room at Northumberland House, London — Howard, op. cit.

[5] Howard, op. cit., p. 157.

[6] Sheraton, *Cabinet Dictionary* (1803), p. 334.

Fig. 68. Knee-hole writing-table, veneered on pine with contre-partie *Boulle marquetry of pewter, brass, copper and shell. Made by Louis Le Gaigneur, c. 1815. Length, 5 ft; depth, 2 ft 11 in.*

1820 they were said to be exhausted.[1] Coromandel wood (from the Coromandel coast of India), resembling and often confused with calamander wood, was but 'lately introduced into England' and said to be 'much in use . . . for banding'.[2] Again, it is close textured, but black in colour, with light brown streaks.

JAPANNED AND PAINTED FURNITURE

The taste for japanned furniture was revived during the Chinese vogue. The term 'japanning' applies properly to work done in imitation of Oriental lacquer. The technique was first described in the *Treatise of Japaning and Varnishing, Being a compleat Discovery of those Arts*, produced by Stalker and Parker in 1688. Japanning methods employed during the Regency were, however, inferior and the equivalent of varnish painting.[3] A lighter and cheaper grade of furniture was made from soft wood japanned, or painted, with a variety of ground colours relieved by designs in contrasting colours, or with *grisaille* picked out in gold. There existed in London a considerable number of 'Japan Chair' manufactories, selling not only seat furniture but card, sofa and toilet tables and various small articles such as 'moving libraries' or bookstands. Bedroom furniture was frequently painted to conform with a decorative scheme. Black was a favourite ground colour, or green in imitation of bronze, especially for furniture in the Grecian taste. According to Ackermann's *Repository of Arts*, in 1809, 'bronze still prevails as a groundwork for chairs, sofas, cabinets, &c., and will always be classic when delicately and sparingly assisted with gold ornaments'. Some painted furniture is found with its ground grained in imitation of the colour and figure of more costly woods. 'Chairs', comments Ackermann's

contributor in 1814, 'may be stained black, or as the present taste is, veined with vitriol, stained with logwood, and polished to imitate rosewood'.

THE INTRODUCTION OF WOODWORKING MACHINERY

At the close of the eighteenth century Sir Samuel Bentham within a few years invented and patented almost every known variety of woodworking machine. Bentham, who was for some years in Russia as a naval architect and engineer, invented shortly after 1779 'the first planing machine for wood that could really be called an organised operating machine',[4] and on his return to England in 1791 devised a large number of woodworking machines for use in convict prisons; his brother Jeremy Bentham's house in Queen's Square, Westminster, was in that year converted into the first manufactory of woodcutting machines. 'In the Bentham factory were made machines for planing, moulding, rebating, grooving, mortising, sawing, in coarse and fine woods, in curved, winding and transverse directions — and shaping wood in all sorts of complicated forms.' In 1791 Samuel Bentham issued his patent for a planing machine, described by him as a 'method of planing divesting the operation of skill previously necessary and a reduction of

---

[1] Maria Edgeworth noticed a table at Aston Hall in 1820 'of wood from Brazil, Zebrawood, and no more of it to be had for love or money' — *Life and Letters* (ed. A. J. C. Hare), Vol. I, p. 256.

[2] Sheraton, op. cit., p. 180.

[3] In *The Artist's Assistant* (1801), japanning 'is understood as the art of covering bodies by grounds of opake colours in varnish, which may be either afterwards decorated by paintings, or left in a plain state'.

[4] *Transactions of the American Society of Mechanical Engineers* (1929).

brute force employed', the suggested motive power being wind, water, steam or animal strength. In 1793 Bentham, in an inclusive patent, originated 'practically every woodworking machine and process that is in use to-day'. Nevertheless, there is no evidence to suggest that such machines were adopted by the cabinet trade during the Regency period. The use of hand tools was continued, even in large workshops, probably until mid-century. The progressive decline in standards of craftsmanship, which is apparent in furniture made after the turn of the century, is more likely to have resulted from the division of labour than the new inventions; many workmen, particularly in the new manufactories, were too narrowly employed in routine processes.

BRASS INLAY AND MARQUETRY, AND METAL WORK

An inlay of fine stringing lines of light coloured wood, such as box or sycamore, was commonly employed as ornament for furniture in the late eighteenth century. From about 1800, the inlay was sometimes of black wood, occasionally disposed in geometrical patterns, or was of brass. Under 'classical' influence simple and isolated *motifs*, including the honeysuckle and palmette, were adopted.

'Brass beads, and small lines of brass', writes Sheraton in 1803, 'are now much in use in the English furniture, and looks [*sic*] very handsome in black, rose and other dark wood grounds. The lines are made of thin sheet brass, which is cut by gages, made by the cabinet-makers for that purpose. The brass beads are fixed to by sharp points soldered to the inside of the bead, which drive into the wood to which the beads are fixed'.[1] Later, he notices this latter as an innovation, and as 'a substantial, though an expensive method of working'.[2] Brass inlay became increasingly popular during the first decade of the century (it was 'durable' and, used with dark woods, extremely decorative) and by 1815 had in large part superseded wood inlay. The inlay of brass (which was not engraved) contrasted with the ground of veneer 'without preventing it by any raised ornaments from being constantly rubbed'.[3] The ornaments, cut out of sheet brass in scroll and floral forms and classical patterns, were inserted into the veneer which was fretted to correspond, and the exactness of finish is admirable. Several drawings for inlay of this character are preserved in a portfolio in the Victoria and Albert Museum, dating from 1816.[4] The woods used as a ground were chosen for a dense, close-grained texture. The presence of this brass inlay on furniture may suggest an origin in London, for such metal work was a specialised trade, carried on in the neighbourhood of St Martin's Lane and Long Acre. As this brass inlay had to be inserted during the progress of cabinet and chair making, it was difficult for country firms, at a distance from metal working centres, to compete in this form of enrichment with the London trade. The technique was not, however, 'a London one alone, for ready-cut brass inlays figure in the pattern-books of Birmingham brass foundries about 1820'.[5]

By 1820, or earlier, ornamentation in brass had entered a second and distinct phase. Patterns in brass were then often exceedingly intricate, and an 'all-over' treatment was favoured. The process may be described as brass marquetry. The decoration derives from, and was directly inspired by, French marquetry furniture, executed in tortoise-shell and brass, in the style of Boulle. The French technique has been described as follows: 'Boulle marquetry is prepared by glueing one or more thin layers of tortoise-shell to the same number of layers of brass. Paper, on which the design of the marquetry was set out, is then pasted on the surface and the pattern cut out by means of a saw. When the cut layers are separated two types of marquetry can be formed by combining the brass and shell, one with the pattern in brass on a ground of shell, known as *première-partie* (first part), and the other with the pattern in shell on a ground of brass, known as *contre-partie* (counterpart or second part). These contrasting marquetries are then applied as veneer on to the carcase which is generally of plain oak. Additional decoration was provided by engraving the brass, and on the finest pieces it is often of a remarkably high quality. . .'[6]

Regency craftsmen followed much the same procedure,[7] except that a combination of brass and wood (usually rosewood or ebony veneers) was used with good effect instead of brass and shell. Brass was contrasted also with woods of lighter tone, such as amboyna or kingwood, which came into fashion during the later Regency. Instances of this are the set of amboyna tables made in 1816 for Princess Charlotte at Claremont (Fig. 66), and a grand piano of walnut made for the Prince Regent about 1818 (Fig. 67), in which the sides of the case and the pedestal support are enriched with large panels of brass marquetry. Alternatively, marquetry furniture employing contrasting light and dark woods was produced. In the golden drawing-room, Carlton House, two circular tables are shown in Pyne's *Royal Residences* 'of Buhl, executed in Rosewood, tortoiseshell and ormolu'.[8] Direct imitations of Boulle furniture, in the style of Louis XIV, were also made in England during the Regency (Fig. 68).[9]

The casting of metals developed in the early nineteenth century, and composition ornament and painting was laid aside as less durable and less 'classic' than applications and inlays of metal. The French and English treatments of applied metal ornament were distinct, the former specialising in chased ormolu mounts — not usually found on English furniture.[10] On a few examples in the Royal Collection, from Deepdene, and at Southill the applied mounts are elaborate and of ormolu, but in such cases a French 'bronzist' may have carried out Hope's and Holland's designs. The mounts on some rosewood bookcases made by Marsh and Tatham are unusually varied, and consist of paterae, entwined rods and the anthemium (Fig. 8). Boileau,[11] a French painter and decorator work-

[1] Op. cit., p. 95.

[2] Op. cit., p. 257.

[3] Hope, *Household Furniture* (1807), p. 35.

[4] One is inscribed 'for Mr Boulton's oak cabinet, 1816'; another, for 'a sofa table' — *Album of Miscellaneous Sketches*.

[5] Brian Reade, *Regency Antiques* (1953), p. 66.

[6] F. J. B. Watson, *Wallace Collection: Catalogue of Furniture* (1956), p. xxiv.

[7] *The Cabinet Maker's Guide* (ed. 1830), by G. A. Siddons contains directions for shell and brass marquetry.

[8] *Royal Residences* (1819), Vol. III, Plate 60.

[9] See 'Records of Furniture Makers'.

[10] Much so-called 'English Ormolu' is in fact brass, lacquered, and not gilt bronze. Gilt metal mounts were used with good effect on furniture of light coloured woods, such as amboyna.

[11] See 'Records of Furniture Makers'.

ing at Carlton House in the 1780's, is later mentioned as being unsurpassed in his designs for casting in ormolu, and possessing 'a light airy and classic style'.[1]

Sheraton expresses the view that French craftsmen depended on 'their superior brass work'. 'If our noblemen and gentry would contribute as much to the encouragement of a national brass foundry, as they do to some other institutions of less consequence, we might have as elegant brass work for cabinets, cast in London, as they have in Paris. It is in this article they excel us, and by which they set off cabinet work; which, without it, would not bear a comparison with ours, neither in design, nor neatness of execution.'[2] There were, however, 'one or two English brass founders in London, not much inferior to the French'.[3]

Brass colonnettes were freely used as supports for galleries and shelves, and brass galleries finished the tops of sideboards, pedestals, secretaires and writing-tables. Cast metal fittings, such as paw feet and handles, are illustrated in catalogues of metal working firms. A tendency to overload furniture with brass is noticed in 1820 as 'frequently seen'.[4] In the words of the *Smelters' and Founders' Director* (1823), this branch of English manufacture was elevated 'far above that of any other country', and raised the articles which were formerly considered as merely 'gross and ponderous into the scale of ornamental embellishment'. This estimate of the advance made during the period may have been optimistic.

POLISH

The preference for smooth glass-like surfaces led to the adoption of 'French' polish, a composition said to have been brought to this country after the peace of 1814, when much furniture unfortunately was stripped and repolished. Formerly, the ordinary polish used by cabinet-makers had consisted of beeswax mixed with spirits of turpentine and some resin. Cold-drawn linseed oil was also used, particularly for dining tables, but the process of polishing was extremely laborious. According to Sheraton the 'plain cabinet work' of his day was commonly treated with linseed oil and brick dust, which formed 'a kind of putty' under the rubbing cloth; by this means a fine

polish was 'infallibly' secured.[5] Such methods had been discontinued in large part by about 1830. Loudon (1833)[6] states that 'in large towns, such as London and Edinburgh, where the art of polishing furniture forms a distinct occupation, what is called the French polish is by far the best for bringing out the beauties of the wood, and giving it a brightness and richness of colour which nothing else hitherto invented can produce'. He recommends its adoption 'at least for all drawing-room furniture, and for the finer articles of libraries and dressing-rooms', on the grounds that 'it is not liable to crack or show scratches, like varnish'. The original 'French' polishing was different from the present — the processes were thorough and lengthy, no stain was then used in the polish and a much better quality of spirit was employed: the grain of the wood was oiled and then filled in carefully with fine powdered pumice and spirit and very highly polished in this state; the 'French' polish (which consisted of different varieties of lac dissolved in spirits of wine) was applied after. Attention was given to the 'spiriting-off' and finishing stages. Richard Brown (1820)[7] advises the following method of making and using 'the French polish':
'Take of mastic one ounce, sandarac one ounce, seed lac one ounce, shell lac one ounce, gum lac one ounce, gum arabic one ounce, and virgin wax quarter of an ounce; these reduce to powder, and put into a bottle with a quart of rectified spirit of wine: after standing some hours, it will be fit for use.

'Make a ball of cloth, and on it occasionally put a little of the polish: afterwards wrap over the ball a piece of calico, which touch on the outside with a little linseed oil; then rub the furniture hard, with a circular motion, until a gloss is produced; finish with one third of the polish to two thirds of the spirit of wine.'

[1] George Smith, *Guide* (1828).
[2] Op. cit., p. 117.
[3] Op. cit., p. 95.
[4] 'There is another very important part in designing furniture in which the cabinet-maker ought to be skilful, that is harmonising metals with woods, so as not to overload the articles with bronze, or ormolu, which is so frequently seen' — Brown, *Rudiments* (1820), p. x.
[5] Op. cit., pp. 289–90.
[6] *Encyclopaedia* (ed. 1835), p. 1063.
[7] Op. cit.

Seat Furniture and Stools

SYDNEY SMITH, reviewing Thomas Hope's *Household Furniture*, points out that it is a 'substantial part' of the convenience of chairs and tables to be easily moved, and that for a great part of the eighteenth century they had become progressively lighter.[1] The cane-seated chairs and settees of painted beech which were in fashion in the late years of the eighteenth century are the lightest phase in this long evolution.[2]

The design of seat furniture then follows with slight modification the traditional form. The arms of chairs are set high in the back uprights, and in most instances are swept up to these near the top, giving a characteristic high-shouldered appearance (Fig. 69). Sometimes arm-supports rise from the side-rails, but for the most part they are continuations of the legs (Fig. 70). Sometimes the arm curves downward in an arc, touching the seat frame and finishing in a small scroll, or is

[1] *Edinburgh Review*, 1807, Vol. X, p. 483.
[2] Sheraton, in 1803, states that about thirty years ago caning had gone out of fashion, but that 'on the revival of japanning furniture, it began to be brought gradually into use, and to a state of improvement' — *Cabinet Dictionary* (1803), p. 126.

Fig. 69. Painted armchair (one of a set of ten), made for Princess Amelia, daughter of George III, and believed to have been used subsequently in the Royal Pavilion, Brighton. The seat rail stamped 'B.T.' and 'I.S.' c. 1800.

Fig. 70. Painted armchair, with caned seat, the panel in centre of the back painted in Pompeian style. The junction of the front legs and arm supports formed by a turned column. c. 1805.

Fig. 71. Mahogany armchair, with lion front legs. c. 1805. Height, 2 ft 10½ in.; width, 2 ft.

Fig. 72. One of a set of 36 chairs, of beech imitating bamboo, in the Oriental taste; supplied by Elward, Marsh and Tatham for the dining room at the Royal Pavilion, Brighton, in 1802, for £71. 'Canvas hair cushions for the back and seats covered with red morocco leather' were charged extra at £132 6s. Height, 2 ft 10 in.; width, 1 ft 4 in.; depth, 1 ft 6 in.

extended in a scroll over the concave arm-support (Fig. 71).

A distinction was drawn between seat furniture made of mahogany or satinwood, and what was termed 'fancy' seat furniture, which was of beech, painted or japanned. An American advertisement by William Challen, in 1797, 'Fancy Chair Maker from London',[1] states that he manufactures 'all sorts of dyed, japanned and bamboo chairs, settees, etc., every article in the fancy chair line executed in the newest and most approved London patterns'. A variety of fancy seat furniture was the bamboo, which was considered suitable for 'rooms slightly decorated'.[2] The imitation of the bamboo, a 'kind of Indian reed', by turning beech into the same form, and painting it to match the colour of the reeds or cane, is described by Sheraton in his *Cabinet Dictionary*.[3] An account of Elward, Marsh and Tatham in 1802 includes 'bamboo chairs japaned and Indian bamboo tables' for the Royal Pavilion at Brighton (Figs. 72 and 73).[4]

In Regency seat furniture the new severity finds expression in the reeding of members, the classic character of the painted decorations and the emphasis upon horizontality in the treatment of the back.

The variety of design is a feature of the period (Figs. 74 and 75), and by 1820 it was said that it 'now baffles the most skilful artists to produce any new forms'.[5]

Exploitation of the antique by Regency designers is reflected as early as 1803 in the *Cabinet Dictionary*. Varieties of arm-chair illustrated by Sheraton include 'Herculaneums' ('so named on account of their antique style of composition'), 'curricles', a tub-shaped chair, an upholstered *fauteuil* with moulded top rail and arms, and a *bergère* with caned back and arms (Figs. 78 and 79).[6] 'Curricles', as they are described by Sheraton, 'from their being shaped like that kind of carriage', were said to be 'well adapted for dining parlours, being of a strong form, easy and conveniently low, affording easier access to a dining table than the common kind'.[7] 'Curricles', which were in fact library chairs, used for reading or writing, were popular throughout the Regency period (Fig. 80). Sheraton figures the lion-leg and the lion-monopodium, which appear

[1] Quoted in Singleton, *Furniture of Our Forefathers*, p. 640.

[2] George Smith, *Household Furniture* (1808), p. 16.   [3] P. 29.

[4] Quoted in H. Clifford Smith, *Buckingham Palace* (1931), p. 112.

[5] R. Brown, *Rudiments* (1820), p. 25.

[6] 'Sometimes the seats are caned, having loose cushions' — p. 19 and Plate 8.   [7] Op. cit., p. 18.

Fig. 73. Caned bergère, *of imitation bamboo, supplied by Elward, Marsh and Tatham for the Royal Pavilion, Brighton, in 1802. Height, 3 ft 3 in.; width, 2 ft 3½ in.; depth, 2 ft 1 in.*

Fig. 74. Painted chair, with spoon back. c. 1810. Height, 2 ft 11½ in.; width, 1 ft 9¾ in.

also in certain examples after George Smith (Figs. 81 and 82), and he gives one design for a conversation chair.

In the type described as reading or conversation chairs, the back is tapered to a narrow waist to allow the occupant to sit astride facing the back. The top rail is flat, to serve as a rest, and in the case of reading chairs is often fitted with folding candle brackets (Fig. 83).

A revolutionary change in design arose from the copying of the Greek chair of the fourth and fifth centuries B.C. (and its Roman derivative). In this chair (κλισμος) the back and rear legs formed a continuous curve, or wide arc, bisected approximately at the level of the seat rail. The in-curving front legs were swept forward to balance. The back was crossed at shoulder height by a broad yoke, of concave form, extending beyond it. Regency 'arc-back' chairs of this type, inspired by the ideal of Grecian severity, were fashionable throughout the period (Figs. 84 and 85). Some chairs were made with straight front legs, either turned or of square section (Figs. 86 and 87).

Sir Walter Scott, writing in 1828, comments on the change of taste: 'An ordinary chair, in the most ordinary parlour, has now something of an antique cast — something of Grecian massiveness, at once, and elegance in its forms. That of twenty or thirty years since was mounted on four tapering and tottering legs, resembling four tobacco-pipes; the present supporters of our stools have a curule air, curve outwards behind, and give a comfortable idea of stability to the weighty aristocrat or ponderous burgess'.[1]

To judge from the variety of surviving specimens, however, the 'scroll-back' chair, distinguished by an outward and backward roll to the top rail, was the type most favoured during the Regency (Figs. 9, 88 and 89).

The well-known 'Trafalgar' chair is of this kind. It was designed as a light 'parlour' chair, and made normally of beech, painted black or green, with caned seat and loose squab cushion, and was in very general production from about 1805. The flowing lines of the chair, particularly when seen in profile, are exceedingly graceful. The sabre-shaped front legs (often with rounded knees) and curved side rails, both of narrow section, are continued into the back uprights and merge smoothly with them (Figs. 90 and 91). The specimen illustrated in Fig. 92 has been adapted to the Chinese taste.

Drawing-room chairs were usually more elaborate and more substantial than those intended for the dining-parlour, and were executed in mahogany or were painted and gilt (Fig. 96). Turned front legs were at no time entirely superseded by swept legs or by animal monopodia, and are in evidence in designs in Hope's *Household Furniture* (1807) and in George Smith's publication in the following year. They returned fully to favour in the later Regency in the heavy coarsened form illustrated by the Nicholsons (1826–7).

A bronze cross-framed seat, drawn by Charles Heathcote Tatham from the original in Rome before 1800, is figured in his

[1] *Quarterly Review*, March 1828.

48

Fig. 75. Painted and bronzed chair. c. *1810.*

Fig. 76. Carved mahogany hall chair; the owner's crest contained within a shield-shaped back, with a honeysuckle ornament prominent below; the feathered front legs finish in eagle ball and claw feet. c. *1805. Height, 2 ft 11 in.*

Fig. 77. Carved mahogany hall seat (one of a pair); the back formed as a classical shield enframed by eagles and connected to the seat by crossed Roman fasces. c. *1805. Width, 2 ft 10 in.*

Fig. 78. Mahogany caned bergère made for Sir Richard Colt Hoare by Thomas Chippendale, the younger, in 1816.

Fig. 79. Mahogany caned bergère. c. 1810.
Height, 3 ft 1½ in.; width, 2 ft 1 in.

Fig. 80. Rosewood ('curricle') armchair, upholstered in leather and
inlaid with brass. c. 1815.

Fig. 81. Painted, bronzed and gilt armchair with caned seat and
sides. From a design, dated 1804, in George Smith's Household
Furniture (1808), Plate 56.

Fig. 82. Painted and gilt armchair, with caned seat and back panel,
the front legs formed as winged lion monopodia. In the manner of
George Smith. c. 1810. Height, 2 ft 9¼ in.; width, 1 ft 10 in.

Fig. 83. *Mahogany library reading and writing chair, in the Gothic taste. According to Sheraton (Cabinet Dictionary, 1803), such chairs were 'intended to make the exercise of reading easy, and for the convenience of taking down a note or quotation from any subject'. The reader placed himself 'with his back to the front of the chair' resting his arms 'on the top yoke'. c. 1820.*

Fig. 84. *'Grecian' chair, with arc back, painted in red and black. In the style of Thomas Hope. c. 1807.*

Fig. 85. *(Below) From Henry Moses'* Designs of modern costume *(1823), Plate 7.*

Fig. 86. *(Right) Satinwood armchair, inlaid with ebony lines, and having a diagonal crossing to the back. Made by Thomas Chippendale, the younger, in 1802 for Sir Richard Colt Hoare.*

Fig. 87. Mahogany single chair, with inlay of black wood. c. 1805. Comparable with a design illustrated by Thomas Hope. Height, 2 ft 8 in.; width, 1 ft 7 in.

Fig. 88. Mahogany upholstered armchair, with carved top rail and arm supports. c. 1805. Height, 3 ft 1½ in.; width, 2 ft 5 in.

Fig. 89. Mahogany armchair, with gilt enrichments. c. 1815. Height, 3 ft; width, 2 ft.

Fig. 90. Satinwood chair, of 'Trafalgar' type, with painted panel on the top rail. c. 1805.

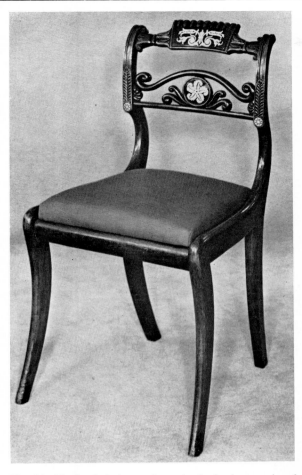

Fig. 91. Single chair (one of a set), the back carved and decorated with brass inlays. Made by J. Gee, c. 1810–15.

Fig. 92. Single chair, japanned black and gold in the Chinese taste. c. 1810. Height, 2 ft 10¾ in.; width, 1 ft 6¾ in.

Fig. 93. Painted single chair (one of a set), the broad concave top rail decorated with musical trophies on a green and brown ground. Made by J. Gee, c. 1810–15.

Fig. 94. One of a set of '8 neat mahogany chairs with fine cane seats', supplied by Gillow's for Broughton Hall, Yorkshire, 1811–13, for 20 guineas.

Fig. 95. Mahogany caned dining chair (one of a large set). c. 1815–20.

Fig. 96. Gilt armchair. c. 1808. Height, 3 ft 2 in.; width, 2 ft 7 in.

Fig. 97. Carved and gilt armchair (one of a set of four), supplied by Morel and Seddon for Windsor Castle in 1828. Height, 3 ft 3 in.

Fig. 98. Richly carved and gilt armchair (one of a set of '6 large elegant bergère chairs, carved chimeras'), supplied by Morel and Hughes for Carlton House in 1812 at a cost of £158 12s. (£951 12s. the set). Height, 3 ft 2 in.

Fig. 99. Carved and gilt chair (part of a set), supported on cabriole legs carved with acanthus. Supplied by Morel and Seddon for Windsor Castle in 1828. Height, 3 ft.

Fig. 100. Carved and gilt armchair (part of a set), supplied by Morel and Seddon for Windsor Castle in 1828. Height, 3 ft 7 in.

Ancient Ornamental Architecture,[1] and close adaptations of this appear in Hope[2] and in Smith.

'Curule' chairs (those with legs composed of double reversed curves, crossed in the centre) enjoyed some popularity. Two arrangements of supports occur, one with the curved legs on both sides joined by a turned stretcher, and the other with curved legs at the front and straight legs at the back. A set of chairs, with only the curved front legs crossing, was made in 1828 by Morel and Seddon for Windsor Castle (Fig. 97).

'Arc-back' armchairs, derived partly from the marble throne, and partly from the French bergère, are reproduced by Hope. At Buckingham Palace is a set of six bergères of this type, caned up to the wide scrolled and upholstered top rail. These were made by Morel and Hughes in 1812, and described in the Royal accounts as 'large elegant bergère chairs, carved chimeras' (Fig. 98).

The design of a pair of throne chairs for use at Royal Councils at Carlton House is based on a Roman type; and one of these (placed by the council table) is clearly shown in a plate in Royal Residences. The backs are carried to the ground and are carved with acanthus scrolls and foliations, and the side supports are in the form of winged sphinxes whose wings form the elbows of the chair (Fig. 11).

During the early nineteenth century there was a revival of the lyre motif for the splat (Fig. 101), and in a contemporary account of an American private yacht (named Cleopatra's

Barge) in 1817, the sofas in the saloon are described as having backs 'shaped like an ancient lyre'.[3]

SETTEES, SOFAS AND COUCHES

The sofa and the settee are distinct articles of furniture, the settee being an extension of the armchair, while the sofa and couch were a development of the day-bed, and adapted for reclining (cf. Figs. 102–4). The term 'couch', according to Sheraton, derived 'from coucher, French, to lie down on a place of repose'. 'Hence', he remarks, 'we have seats and beds that bear this name.'[4] The couch was fashionable by reason of its being an article associated with classical antiquity. The classic couch dominated the design of the Regency and of the contemporary French Empire. When Madame Recamier was painted by David in 1800,[5] the couch on which she is shown seated is of classic type, resting on supports consisting of many-membered turnings.

[1] Ed. 1803, Plate 75.

[2] Described as 'antique seats from bronze originals at Rome'. Plate 20, described in the text as 'an armchair after the manner of the ancient curule chairs'.

[3] Salem Gazette, January, 1817. A contemporary account of the yacht, quoted by G. Singleton, Furniture of Our Forefathers, p. 555, describes them in fuller detail: 'The sofas in the cabin were of mahogany and birds'-eye maple, and measured eleven feet in length. The lyres forming the back were strung with thick brass wire'.   [4] Op. cit., p. 182.

[5] Portrait in the Louvre.

Fig. 101. Caned mahogany sofa. c. 1820. Height, 2 ft 10 in.; length, 8 ft.

Fig. 102. Mahogany and gilt hall settee (one of a pair), painted with the Royal arms and the Prince of Wales' Feathers; made by Elward, Marsh and Tatham, probably from a design by Holland, for the Royal Pavilion, Brighton, in 1802. The settees cost £56 14s. Length, 7 ft.

Fig. 103. Settee of grained rosewood, with gilt enrichments, covered with contemporary needlework, c. 1805. Length, 5 ft 6 in.; depth, 2 ft 3 in.; height of back, 2 ft 10 in.

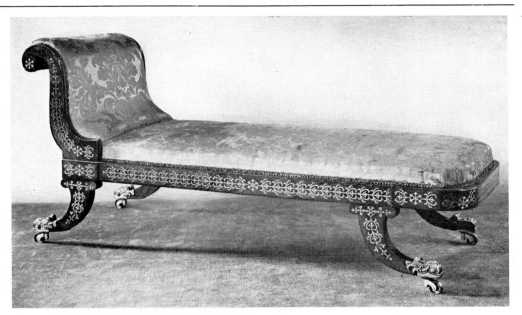

Fig. 104. Rosewood couch, with ornamental brass inlay. c. 1810.

Fig. 105. Couch (one of a pair), japanned black and gold. c. 1800. Height, 2 ft 9 in.; length, 5 ft.

Fig. 106. Painted sofa. c. 1810. Height, 2 ft 10 in.; length, 7 ft.

57

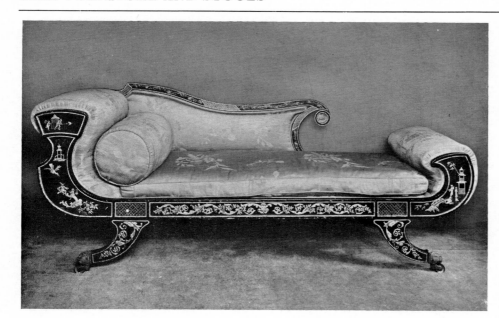

Fig. 107. Painted sofa of couch form, with gilt enrichments. c. 1815.

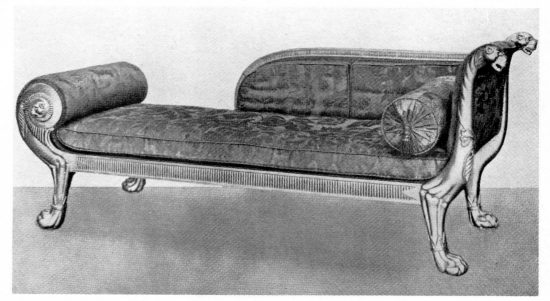

Fig. 108. Sofa of couch form, of carved and gilt wood, the uprights at the head formed as lion terminals and the scrolled end carved with lion masks, with lion supports. Part of a set made by Gillow's in 1805. Height, 2 ft 8½ in.; length, 6 ft 8 in.

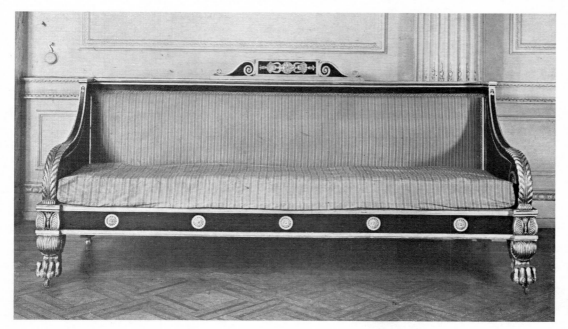

Fig. 109. Sofa, with carved and gilt details. c. 1825. Height, 3 ft; length, 6 ft 4½ in.

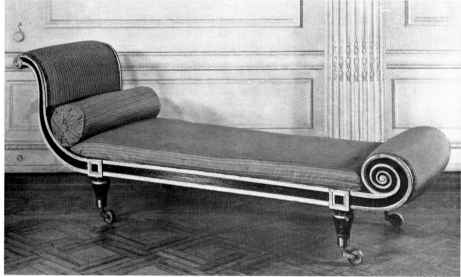

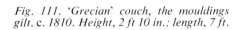

Fig. 110. Gilt couch (one of a pair). c. 1800. Described in the inventory of Southill, taken in 1815, as 'a single-head couch'.

Fig. 111. 'Grecian' couch, the mouldings gilt. c. 1810. Height, 2 ft 10 in.; length, 7 ft.

Fig. 112. Carved rosewood 'window sofa', with decorative panels of brass marquetry. c. 1820. Length, 4 ft 2 in.

Fig. 113. 'Grecian' cross-framed gilt stool. c. *1810.*

Fig. 114. Gilt cross-framed seat. c. *1805.*

In designs by Sheraton, a 'Grecian couch' has a head, a short arm rest and low foot-piece, whereas a 'Grecian sofa' is shown with identical ends and with a straight, comparatively high back.[1] The demand for both types persisted for more than a quarter of a century (Figs. 105 and 106). The supports were variously swept, short and top-shaped, or in the form of lion feet (Figs. 107 and 108). The heavy, turned leg is usually a late feature, as is also the central cresting that figures on the back rail of double-ended sofas from about 1810 onwards (Fig. 109). The 'single-head couch' was also a popular form of seat (Figs. 110 and 111). The fantastic piece in the form of a crocodile (Fig. 37) — which preserves its original bluish-green colouring, with flutings and mouldings picked out in gold — is described in an inventory of 1820 as 'an antique or Grecian couch with crocodile legs'.[2]

Sheraton[3] recommends the furnishing of a drawing-room with two sofas, to be covered with figured silk or satin, and to have 'cushions to fit their backs, together with bolsters at each end'; sets of two sofas are to be found at Southill. In the drawing-room illustrated and described by George Smith (1808), four sofas are grouped round a centre table; they are described in Ackermann's *Repository of Arts*, 1809, as 'an indispensable article of furniture' in a library. They are hinted at as a relaxation after an exhausting day in Jane Austen's *Mansfield Park*, when the guests at a picnic in the grounds of Sotherton 'returned to the house together there to lounge away the time as they could with sofas and chitchat'. In modest households their use by the younger members of the family was resented by their elders, and Mrs Norris complains that it is 'a shocking trick for a young person to be always lolling on a sofa'. There would often be but one in the house, and in less luxurious households, to lie down, or even to lean back, was a luxury permitted only to old persons and invalids. Sofas are instanced by Cobbett among the innovations that accompanied the increased wealth of the tenant farmer, who was able to afford a fox-hunting horse and polished boots, as well as a house 'crammed up with sofas, pianos, and all sorts of fooleries'. The vogue for sofas or settees is shown by the large proportion of these to chairs in a set of seat furniture made for Windsor Castle in 1828.

THE OTTOMAN

The ottoman (or Turkey sofa), a long and low upholstered seat,[4] without back or ends, is described by Sheraton as a fashionable novelty in 'imitation of the Turkish mode of sitting', and is shown by him, in his illustration of the Chinese Room at Carlton House, as extending the whole width of the room. George Smith defines it as a long couch, which should be placed on the chimney side of the room with a similar seat or seats on the opposite side.

WINDOW STOOLS, STOOLS AND FOOTSTOOLS

The small window benches or stools which were set in window recesses are closely related to designs for chairs, their ends being reduced replicas of chair backs.

Stools serving as 'ornamental centre seats in elegant rooms' continued to be made as adjuncts to large sets of seat furniture for state rooms. The many and various stools of cross-framed design are especially graceful (Figs. 113–16). A long stool, with gilt enrichments, at the Town Hall, Liverpool (Fig. 117), resembles a type figured in George Smith's *Household Furniture* (1808), and is referred to as a 'Tête-à-Tête Seat'.

Among the novel features in the design of footstools is the appearance of scrolled ends, rising above the upholstered surface, giving the piece the appearance of a miniature couch (Fig. 118). In another design the anthemium is applied to the four angles (Fig. 9). A stool in the form of an S-shaped scroll, covered on the upper face, is also figured in Ackermann's *Repository of Arts*.

[1] Op. cit., Plates 49, 73.

[2] *Country Life*, May 10, 1930.

[3] *Drawing-Book* (1791–4). Sheraton does not draw any distinction between the settee and the sofa. He refers to both articles as 'sofas'.

[4] 'The modern ottoman may be more elegant than the old sofa, but an old and infirm person is very apt to tumble backwards from it' — *Anecdotes and Egotisms of Henry Mackenzie (1745–1831)* (ed. 1927), p. 14.

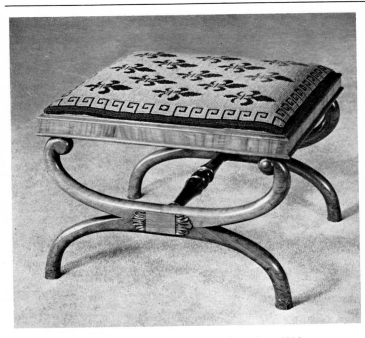

Fig. 115. *Mahogany cross-framed stool*. c. 1800. *Height, 1 ft 3½ in.; length, 1 ft 9 in.*

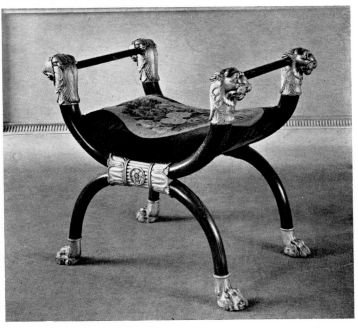

Fig. 116. *Painted cross-framed seat, with gilt enrichments. From a design in Thomas Hope's* Household Furniture *(1807), Plate 12. Height, 2 ft 4 in.*

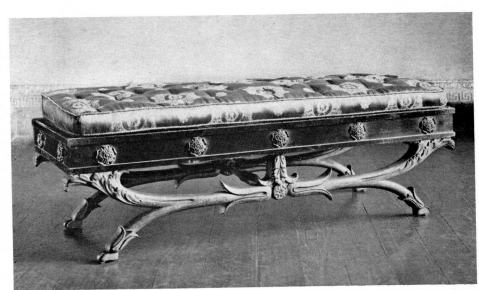

Fig. 117. *Long stool with gilt enrichments; the supports gilt.* c. 1810. *Height, 1 ft 6 in.; length, 3 ft 10 in.*

Fig. 118. *Mahogany footstool of couch form.* c. 1800. *Height, 9½ in.; length, 1 ft 4½ in.*

Tables

TABLES, structurally, fall into three types: the first supported by legs at the corners; the second, on a central pillar or pedestal; the third, at the ends.

'CLASSICAL' TABLES
A table with a round or octagonal top and supported by a central shaft, or by animal legs, was revived (Figs. 119 and 120). Another type of table was provided with a splayed central support; one of this form (Fig. 20),[1] heavily inlaid with ebony and silver, was made for Thomas Hope, and figures in his *Household Furniture*.

Side-tables are given prominence in the *Drawing Book* (1791–4), and their tops, as Sheraton notes, were sometimes of solid marble. The use of marble slabs was carried on into the nineteenth century, when the design of many of these tables (and articles of furniture of comparable form) incorporated lion monopodia, or Egyptian terminal figures (Figs. 122–4).

A looking-glass plate was often placed at the back for the sake of the reflection (Fig. 126). Examples of the finished classical furniture of this period are the pier-tables at Windsor Castle,[2] each surmounted by a slab of verde-antique marble and supported at either end by seated gryphons which were made originally for Carlton House. The gryphon *motif* dominates the design of the gilt side-table illustrated in Fig. 127.

DINING-TABLES
During the second half of the eighteenth century, the large dining-table was built up of units and described as a 'set of dining-tables'. These units consisted of two end tables, each with four fixed legs and D-shaped, rectangular or semi-circular top, and a central unit with rectangular flaps supported on gate-legs. The flaps were attached to each other by means of

[1] Included in the Deepdene sale, July, 1917.
[2] Sir G. Laking, *The Furniture of Windsor Castle* (1905), Plate 23.

Fig. 119. *Octagonal rosewood table; the top of inlaid marble. The lion monopodia are parcel-gilt, the frieze and platform mounted with brass. c. 1810. Height, 2 ft 7 in.; width, 2 ft 1½ in.*

Fig. 120. *Circular table veneered with zebra wood, with gilt paw feet. c. 1810. Height, 2 ft 5 in.; diameter of top, 4 ft.*

Fig. 121. Circular table, with inlaid marble top rimmed with ormolu; the tripod support of carved and gilt wood. c. 1825. Diameter of top, 2 ft 2 in.

Fig. 122. Mahogany side-table (one of a pair), with frieze inlaid with ebonised ornament. c. 1810.

Fig. 123. (Above) Dining-room side-table (one of a set). c. 1800.

Fig. 124. (Right) Mahogany pier-table (or dwarf bookcase), supported by winged lion monopodia. c. 1810. Height, 3 ft 1 in.; length, 5 ft.

Fig. 125. Top of console table (Fig. 126).

Fig. 126. Console table, supported by carved gilt lion monopodia, the top formed of a slab of scagliola (Fig. 125). c. 1810. Height, 2 ft 11 in.; length, 4 ft 1½ in.

Fig. 127. Gilt side-table, with gryphon supports.

Fig. 128. Table, veneered with coromandel wood and parcel gilt; supported on end standards. c. 1810.

Fig. 129. Mahogany dining-table, with three tripod supports. c. 1825.

brass clips and sockets. Such tables are rarely met with complete, as their component sections have often been separated, and regarded as side- or smaller dining-tables. In a letter written in 1800, Jane Austen writes of one of these composite tables that had just arrived: 'The two ends put together form one constant table for everything, and the centre piece stands exceedingly well under the glass, and holds a great deal most commodiously without looking awkwardly.'[1] Some very large composite tables were made, and in Gillow's Cost books for 1795 is a sketch of a table in ten sections, measuring twenty-four feet in length.

A variant support was a central pillar, supported by four 'claws', and in Sheraton's illustration of the dining-parlour at Carlton House there is shown 'a large range of dining-tables, standing on pillars with four claws each, which is now the fashionable way of making these tables'.[2] 'Pillar-and-Claw' tables soon became very popular; they form a majority, perhaps, of dining-tables made during the Regency period. Sheraton, some years later, names the type as 'common' and

'useful' and states that tables may be made 'to any size, by having a sufficient quantity of pillar and claw parts, for between each of these is a loose flap, fixed by means of iron straps and buttons, so that they are easily taken off and put aside; and the beds may be joined to each other with brass fork or strap fastenings'. He allows '2 feet to each person sitting at table' and suggests that a single table for eight persons should measure '5 feet by 4', or a little less, 'at which two upon each side may sit'.[3] In some later examples the supporting pedestal rises from a platform base, or plinth, often of triangular form, with paw or scrolled feet at the angles (Fig. 129).

In the year 1800 a patent was taken out for extending tables by Richard Gillow. His improvement (known as the Patent Imperial dining-table) consisted of 'attaching to a table mounted upon a frame and legs or a pillar and claws, wooden

[1] J. E. Austen-Leigh, *A Memoir of Jane Austen*, p. 58.
[2] *Drawing Book* (1791–4), p. 440.
[3] *Cabinet Dictionary* (1803), pp. 195–6.

Fig. 130. 'Set of ma-hogany Imperial dining tables on stout twined reeded legs and brass socket casters', supplied by Gillow's for Broughton Hall, Yorkshire, in 1813. The table, which is of a type patented by Gillow's in 1800, together with a 'painted rack lined with green baize to contain the leaves' cost 50 guineas.

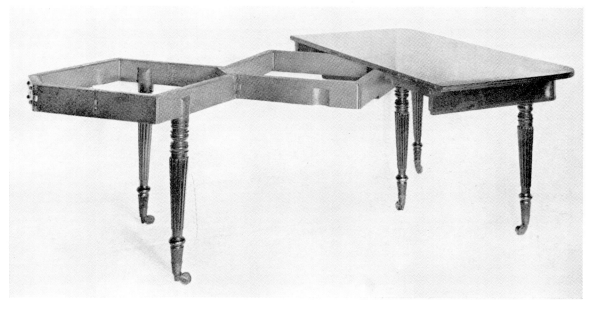

Fig. 131. Mahogany dining-table, with extend-ing frame (part of the top removed). Made by Sed-don's, c. 1810.

or metal sliders which run in dovetail, T or square or cylindrical or other grooves, with or without wheels or rollers'.[1] These sliders are drawn out to the length required and flaps are laid upon them (Fig. 130).

In another form of extending table, the movable part, when drawn out, forms a lazy tongs, and the legs, of which there are two to each division of the tongs, are 'fixed in joints made of brass, iron, or any other suitable materials'[2] (Fig. 131).

In the case of extending round tables with a central support, shaped sections are added forming an outer border, fixed by long bearers and kept rigid by brackets. Sometimes an addi-tional outer section is added. A later expanding table is con-structed so that the sections composing its surface may be caused to diverge from a common centre, and that the spaces caused thereby may be filled up by inserting leaves or 'filling' pieces. 'The expansion may be by hand or by turning the surface and bed of the table round the pillar'.[3]

The heavier supports characteristic of the second decade of the nineteenth century are shown in a dining-table at Liverpool Town Hall, in which the bases of the stout columns are carved with acanthus. By 1835 an 'excessive breadth' was fashionable, for 'the purpose of holding first the cumbrous ornaments and lights, secondly in some cases the dessert, at the same time with the side dishes'.[4]

The round dining-table was revived in the first years of the nineteenth century. A visitor to Cobham Hall in 1804 observed that 'they dine at a *round* table, Lord Darnley sometimes sitting in one part & sometimes in another, & Lady Darnley always on His right hand'.[5] The advantage of the circular form was, we are told,[6] 'to avoid distinction in guests'. The round table in Jane Austen's novel *Emma* (published in 1816), is described as the 'modern' table which had superseded the Pembroke, 'upon which all Mr Woodhouse's meals had been crowded'.

[1] *Abridgements of Specifications*, Vol. 39.
[2] George Remington's patent, December, 1807.
[3] Robert Jupe's patent, March, 1835.
[4] The *Original*, September 2, 1835.
[5] *Farington Diary*, March 10, 1804.
[6] Ackermann's *Repository of Arts*, July, 1827.

Fig. 132. Sofa table, with lyre supports, the ground stained black
leaving the ornament in the natural white wood. c. 1810.
Height, 2 ft 4½ in.; length, 4 ft 11½ in.

Fig. 133. Rosewood sofa table, banded with satinwood and resting on
lyre supports. Made by Thomas Chippendale, the younger, in 1802 for
Sir Richard Colt Hoare. Height, 2 ft 5 in.; length (extended), 5 ft 6 in.

Fig. 134. Zebra wood sofa table. Made in 1810 by George Oakley.
See Fig. 157. Height, 2 ft 3½ in.; length (extended), 5 ft.

Fig. 135. Kingwood sofa table, made by Semple's in 1809 ('a fine kingwood sopha table with orangewood border. 2 Drawers on solid turned
standards & Rich Brass Lions paws & scroll castors. the whole superbly
ornamented with ormolu mouldings. £22'). Height, 2 ft 4 in.; length
(extended), 4 ft 10½ in.

PEMBROKE AND SOFA TABLES

The table described as a 'Pembroke', having flaps at the sides,
supported on hinged wooden brackets, was widely used early
in the reign of George III[1] and continued in fashion during the
Regency. In Jane Austen's unfinished fragment, *The Watsons*
(written about 1803–4), the Pembroke serves as a tea-table —
'people . . . arranged with all the honours of visiting round the
fire, and Miss Watson seated at the best Pembroke table, with
the best tea-things before her'.

A longer table, the sofa table, with end flaps, was also constructed with fly brackets, and Sheraton describes such tables as
'used before a sofa' and 'generally made between 5 and 6 feet
long, and from 22 inches to 2 feet broad'. Ladies (it is added)
'chiefly occupy them to draw, write or read upon'.[2] The junction
of the flap and centre section in these tables is rule-jointed, and
there is a drawer or drawers in the frieze.

A variety of patterns was employed for the supports, ranging
from end-standards (Figs. 132 and 133) and a pedestal (or
balusters) resting on a platform supported by splayed legs, as in

the examples made in the second decade of the nineteenth
century (Figs. 66 and 134).

In the later Regency sofa tables were made without flaps
(*cf*. Figs. 138 and 139). George Smith in his *Guide* (1828), draws
no distinction between the sofa table and the occasional table.

OCCASIONAL TABLES, NESTS OF TABLES

'Little tables placed in every direction' were counted among the
modern and confusing additions to an old-fashioned parlour,[3]
and there exist many small portable tables which were used to
set about the rooms to hold lights, needlework, or papers.
'I think', writes Fanny Burney to her father, 'no room looks
really comfortable, or even quite furnished, without two tables
— one to keep the wall and take upon itself the dignity of a

[1] A Pembroke table of mahogany was supplied by Thomas Chippendale
to Nostell Priory on June 24, 1766. The earliest use of the word given in the
New English Dictionary appears in 1778.

[2] *Cabinet Dictionary* (1803), pp. 305–6.

[3] In Jane Austen's *Persuasion*, finished in 1816, published 1818.

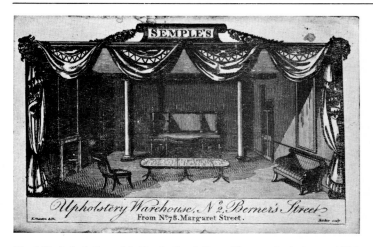

Fig. 136. J. & A. Semple's Trade Card. From Sheraton's design, c. 1805.

Fig. 137. Rosewood sofa table, with decorative brass inlay, on central U-shaped support. c. 1815. Length (extended), 4 ft 11 in.

Fig. 138. Centre table of maple wood, with carved and gilt supports and brackets. c. 1810. Height, 2 ft 4½ in.; length, 4 ft 10½ in.

Fig. 139. Mahogany table, the top decorated in pen and ink on a prepared ground, and dated 1815. Height, 2 ft 4¼ in.; length, 5 ft 1¾ in.

Fig. 140. Table, with rosewood top (mounted with a brass gallery) and base, and painted bamboo supports. c. 1810.

Fig. 141. Occasional table, the top of 'plum-pudding' mahogany bound with brass and containing a panel of pietre dure (a mosaic of hard stones including lapis lazuli, malachite and onyx), of Florentine origin; the columnar rosewood supports mounted with ormolu and decorated with upright leaves and reeding. c. 1800. Height, 2 ft 3½ in.; length, 2 ft 8½ in.

Fig. 142. Painted tripod table (dated 1805 on top).

Fig. 143. Occasional table (one of a pair), with kingwood top and brass gallery; the centre support gilt and carved in the Egyptian taste. c. 1810–15. Height, 2 ft 5 in.

Fig. 144. Occasional table of amboyna, with decorative inlay of brass; the columnar support based on a platform and claws. c. 1815.

Fig. 145. Set of mahogany 'quartetto' tables; the tops inlaid with brass stars. Made by George Oakley for Papworth Hall in 1810. Height (enclosed), 2 ft 5 in.; width, 1 ft 6 in.

Fig. 146. Rosewood work-box on stand. c. 1810.

Fig. 147. Pedestal work- or pouch-table, ebonised and decorated with scrolling designs in penwork. The banding to the tray top, and the handles, of Sheffield plate. c. 1810.

Fig. 148. Work-table, veneered with burr maple, with platform base on bun feet; the end flaps supported by scrolled brackets. c. 1820–30. Width (extended), 2 ft 6 in.

little tidyness, the other to stand here, there, and everywhere, and hold letters and *make the agreeable*.'[1]

Small oblong tables of rosewood, satinwood and mahogany supported at either end by columnar legs resting on splayed feet were common in the early nineteenth century. Fig. 140 shows a specimen with slender supports of painted 'bamboo' rising from a low platform. Two tables from Southill have end-supports; they are usually elegant of form, enriched with gilding and mounted with ormolu (Figs. 7 and 141). A number of small tables are of tripod form (Fig. 142); a small monopodium at Southill, one of a pair, has as its centre support a reeded column springing from a lotus-calyx (Fig. 143).

Nests of four tables of graduated size, which are illustrated in Sheraton's *Cabinet Dictionary*, were known as 'quartetto tables',[2] and are defined as 'a kind of small work table made to draw out of each other, and may be used separately, and again enclosed within each other when not wanted' (Fig. 145).[3] The slender legs were often turned in imitation of bamboo. Some quartetto tables were, later, constructed with lyre-shaped supports.

WORK-TABLES

The work-table differs from the small occasional table in often having a lifting top disclosing a well or small drawers. In many of these tables a bag or pouch is affixed to a sliding frame. The pouch table is defined by Sheraton[4] as a 'Table with a Bag, used by the ladies to work at, in which bag they deposit their fancy needlework'. The work bags 'are suspended to a frame which draws forward'. Work-tables and boxes exist in considerable variety (Figs. 146–50).

A work-table formed as a globe on a stand was among the innovations of the period. A work-table of this description, having the quarters of the globe divided by fine stringing lines of holly meeting at the top in a brass patera, is in The Lady Lever Art Gallery (Fig. 151). When open it discloses a small temple backed by looking-glass, and fitted with columns and chequered parquet floor, and having numerous small drawers and receptacles for work. The legs supporting the globe are united by a galleried bowl to contain the odds and ends of needlework. A second table of this form is in the Royal collection (Fig. 152).

A combined games and work-table was in use in the early nineteenth century, which has the reversible top or a slide inlaid with a chess- or backgammon-board (Fig. 153).

[1] Letter, September 6, 1801, quoted in Constance Hill's *Juniper Hall* (1904), pp. 258–9.
[2] Quartetto = quartet, a set of four things.
[3] P. 293.   [4] Op. cit., p. 292.

Fig. 149. Mahogany work-table, supported on end standards, which are elaborately carved. c. 1825.

Fig. 150. Ovate work-box, of mahogany inlaid with satinwood and olivewood, supported by carved figures resting on a circular base. c. 1795.

Fig. 153. Calamander wood combined work- and games-table, fitted with a pouch, and with slide designed for use as a chess-board. c. *1800. Height, 2 ft 5½ in.; length, 2 ft 6 in.*

Fig. 151. Mahogany work-table of the same type as that illustrated in Fig. 152. The supports united by a galleried bowl, purposed to contain the odds and ends of needlework. The top falls back to disclose a fitted interior, with recessed temple niche, backed by looking glass, with chequered parquet floor. c. *1810. Height, 3 ft.*

Fig. 152. Mahogany globe-shaped work-table, decorated with the signs of the Zodiac engraved on a band of ebony; the legs of ebonised wood, parcel gilt. Bought by Queen Charlotte as a birthday gift for the Princess Augusta in 1810. Height, 3 ft.

Fig. 154. Rosewood card table (one of a pair), in the Egyptian taste; the top cross-banded with satinwood, the legs bronzed, with gilt enrichments. c. *1805–10. Length, 3 ft 1 in.*

Fig. 155. Mahogany card table (one of a pair), inlaid on top and frieze; the standard partly decorated with gilding, and the feet bronzed. c. *1810. Height, 2 ft 4½ in.; length, 3 ft.*

Fig. 156. Rosewood card table, with folding top and carved and gilt dolphin supports; part of a large suite of gilt furniture made by William Collins and presented to Greenwich Hospital in 1813 by the widow of Mr John Fish, in memory of Lord Nelson. Height, 2 ft 5½ in.; length, 3 ft 2 in.

Fig. 157. Card table of calamander wood, inlaid with brass and ebony. Made by George Oakley in 1810. See Fig. 134.

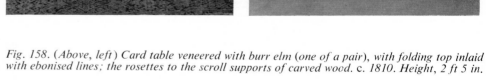

Fig. 158. (Above, left) Card table veneered with burr elm (one of a pair), with folding top inlaid with ebonised lines; the rosettes to the scroll supports of carved wood. c. 1810. Height, 2 ft 5 in.

Fig. 159. (Above, centre) Rosewood card table, with ornamental brass inlay. c. 1815. Length, 3 ft.

Fig. 160. (Above, right) Rosewood card table, with gilt enrichments, decorated with brass marquetry and inlay, and applied metal ornaments; the end supports of scrolled outline are tied by a turned stretcher centring in a lotus leaf motif and rest on stylised paw feet. In the style of Louis Le Gaigneur. c. 1815. Length, 3 ft; depth, 1 ft 6 in.

Fig. 161. (Left) Rosewood table, with semi-circular ends upheld by scrolled brackets and fitted with brass gallery, supported on standards; simulated bamboo mouldings and an ornamental turning filling the standards are distinctive decorative features. c. 1810. Length, 3 ft 9 in.

Fig. 162. Circular table, of rosewood, with decorative brass inlay; the winged paw feet gilt. c. 1815. Height, 2 ft 4½ in.; diameter of top, 3 ft 9 in.

Fig. 163. Design for a 'Circular Table', from the Nicholsons' Practical Cabinet Maker (1826–7), Plate 69.

GAMES TABLES

Fewer card tables appear to have been made in the Regency period, but there was a revival of the combined games and card table. This type has a centre with lifting top, having a back-gammon-board on one side and a chess-board on the other. Card tables were constructed with hinged folding tops and, when not in use for play, served as wall pieces. The supports found in surviving specimens are of the several types that have been noted (Figs. 154–60). 'This ornamental piece of furniture', writes Smith, 'will admit of every variety in execution.'[1]

LOO TABLES

Loo tables, although designed specifically for the round game of cards, known originally as 'lanterloo', which came into favour in England in the later eighteenth century,[2] were put to general use. They were centre tables, usually of circular form and of substantial, but convenient size (Figs. 55 and 162). Sheraton gives a design for a large loo table in the *Cabinet Dictionary*.[3] This is not typical in that it has a rectangular top and is supported on an enclosed cupboard base, resting on paw

feet. A table made in 1810 for Papworth Hall and described in George Oakley's account as 'a calamanderwood circular loo table upon pedestal and claws, the top inlaid with a border of stars in brass and ebony' is more representative of those supplied in the early years of the nineteenth century. Both Brown (*Rudiments*, 1820) and Smith (*Guide*, 1828) illustrate a circular loo table with massive central support (a pillar or a triangular pedestal with concave sides) resting on a base with three or four feet. Smith's 'Octangular Tent Room', designed as 'a morning room for the receiving of visitors' and to make one of a suite of apartments for evening assemblies, contains a loo table with octagonal top. The table (to be made of rosewood, with gilt enrichments) is set prominently in the centre of the room. The Nicholsons' design for a 'Circular Table' (Fig. 163) is markedly individual in style, and the luxuriant character of the leaf ornament at the base is pronounced.

[1] *Household Furniture* (1808).
[2] In Charlotte Smith's *Ethelinda* (1789), Vol. II, p. 132: 'Dinner was no sooner over than the loo table was introduced into the drawing-room'.
[3] P. 338, and Plate 58. The top measures 6 ft 9 ins by 4 ft 6 ins.

Library and Writing-Tables

THE accepted type of pedestal writing-table, with a central knee-hole flanked by cupboards, gave little scope for variation except in detail, but the lion support and *motifs* from the Egyptian style are introduced in the early nineteenth century. In the table made in 1805 for Stourhead by the younger Thomas Chippendale, the round ends are supported by what the maker describes as 'therms with Egyptian heads', while the engaged terms flanking the pedestals finish in classical heads (Fig. 34).

Examples of classical treatment are a pedestal table (Fig. 164), with its panelled doors mounted with bronze reliefs of the Athenian owl, and Greek characters within a laurel wreath, and frieze inlaid with a Greek fret in brass on an ebony ground; and a table in the Victoria and Albert Museum which has its cupboards flanked by caryatid terms, and frieze, sides and panels carved in low relief with classical *motifs* (Fig. 165). Desks, or writing-tables of this type, fitted with pedestals of drawers, unenclosed by doors, exhibit a greater diversity of form (Figs. 166 and 167).

The Carlton House table bore this name very soon after its introduction, but there is no evidence in the Royal accounts that it was made for the Prince of Wales's London house. It is a table with drawers in the frieze and a superstructure extending round the sides and back and fitted with small drawers and cupboards. A sketch of a 'Carleton House table' appears in Gillow's Cost books for 1796. The superstructure is stepped at each side, and this design is repeated in the Cost books two years later (1798) for the Earl of Derby. In several examples the sides are carried up to the level of the back. The first suggestion of the Carlton House type is a design in Sheraton's *Appendix* to his *Drawing Book* (1793) described as a 'Lady's Drawing and

Writing table', differing only from the usual pattern in having a rising desk in the middle to slide forward. A variant is the example from Hinchingbrooke, with its superstructure of even height (Fig. 168). In some Carlton House tables the legs have a tassel capping similar to a rosewood writing-table at Buckingham Palace dating from about 1813. The type was long lived, and remained in fashion for many years.

Tambour and cylinder fronted writing-tables continued to be made. A tambour writing-table from Southill (Fig. 4) is veneered with rosewood and surmounted by a white marble top. The brackets between the legs and the underframing and the capping on the legs are of ormolu. A cylinder writing-table, resting on end supports with splayed feet is illustrated in the *Cabinet Dictionary*; intended 'to stand in the centre of a room, it is made to appear alike on each side' (Fig. 170). Shallow rectangular tables carried on curved, cross-shaped end supports, or standards, having usually a drawer or drawers in the frieze, are among the most attractive of Regency productions.

A new pattern was the table with a revolving circular top in which the deep frieze is fitted with drawers. This pattern appears in Gillow's Cost books in 1795, and is described as 'a round mahogany library table'. As the top revolved, each drawer could be brought in front of the writer. Tables of this variety with a polygonal top were also widely made. The specimen in Fig. 171 is provided with hinged sections to the top. The centre support ranges from the pillar and claw to the massive column resting on a flat base (Fig. 172). In a composite piece (Fig. 173), the base of the table is shelved and protected by a trellis of brass wire.

Writing-tables with a drawer or drawers in the frieze only

Fig. 164. Mahogany pedestal library table, with applied bronze enrichments; the frieze inlaid in brass on an ebony ground. c. 1805. Length, 7 ft.

Fig. 165. Pedestal library table of mahogany, veneered with sabicu; with carved frieze, enrichments on the panels and terminal figures. c. 1810. Height, 2 ft 7 in.; length, 8 ft.

Fig. 166. Mahogany pedestal library table resembling a design for 'a new shaped library table' in Sheraton's Cabinet Dictionary (1803), Plate 56.

Fig. 167. Olivewood pedestal writing-table or desk; the shelved superstructure and mounts of ormolu. c. 1815.

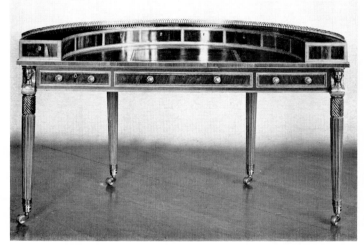

Fig. 168. Rosewood table of Carlton House type; the Egyptian heads of brass. c. 1807.

Fig. 169. Writing-table of rosewood, banded with satinwood, with gilt metal enrichments; the receptacles at the ends each fitted with two drawers; the knee-hole flanked by two tiers of three drawers (and, on the reverse side, two deep drawers). All faces are masked as drawers with ivory fittings. c. 1805. Length, 3 ft 10 in.; depth, 1 ft 11 in.

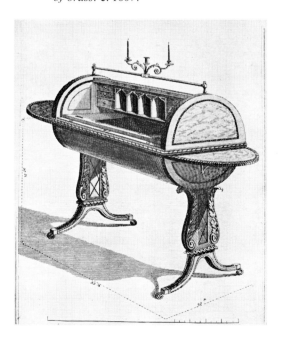

Fig. 170. Design for 'A Lady's Cylinder Writing-Table', from Sheraton's Cabinet Dictionary (1803), Plate 38.

Fig. 171. Mahogany table, having hinged sections to the top. c. 1800.

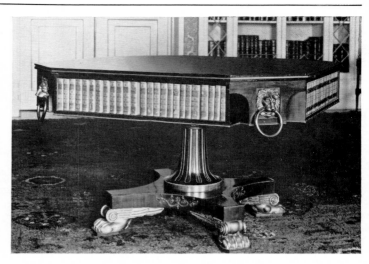

Fig. 172. Rosewood library table, with brass ring handles, the frieze fitted for books, the winged paw feet gilt. c. 1820.

Fig. 173. Maplewood table and bookcase, with bronzed enrichments. Height, 2 ft 6½ in.; diameter of top, 3 ft.

Fig. 174. Rosewood writing-table, with bronzed legs. c. 1800.

Fig. 175. Rosewood table, fitted with a brass gallery. c. 1800. Height, 2 ft 7¾ in.; length, 3 ft 4 in.

Fig. 176. Rosewood table, mounted with gilt brass busts at the angles. c. 1805. Height, 2 ft 6½ in.; length, 3 ft.

II. Writing-table, veneered with walnut and burr maple.

were also very popular; they are carried on end supports and stylistically bear a close resemblance to sofa tables (Figs. 174–9 and Plate II). Fig. 180, a table with semi-circular ends, has scrolled legs, headed by lion masks, at the four corners.

THE DAVENPORT

The name given to a small and compact writing desk of distinctive pattern (a case of drawers surmounted by a desk), in popular use throughout the first half of the nineteenth century. A piece of this kind is said first to have been made by Gillow's for a Captain Davenport in the 1790's and repeat orders for Davenport desks subsequently appear in the firm's records. Loudon[1] remarks 'Devonports [sic] (so called from the inventor's name)' are drawing-room pieces and 'very useful articles

for industrious young ladies'. They may stand in the middle of a room. The Davenport is usually so constructed that the top part (the desk or writing slope) pulls forward over the knees of the user for the convenience of writing; the drawers, and often a slide (for papers, a candle etc.), are contained on the right-hand side. Corresponding drawers on the other side, or sides, are sham. Specimens with columnar or scroll supports enframing a panelled front or sham drawers, and resting often on a low plinth, appear to date from 1820 onwards.

Examples of the small *bonheur-du-jour*, a lady's table of a type that was popular in the late eighteenth century, were also produced at this period (Fig. 182).

[1] *Encyclopaedia* (ed. 1835), p. 1065.

Fig. 177. Table, veneered with zebra wood. c. 1810–15.

Fig. 178. Rosewood writing-table, with brass mounts; the form and filling of the standards is distinctive. Compare with Fig. 161. c. 1815. *Length, 3 ft 10 in.*

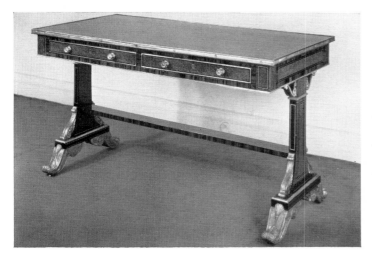

Fig. 179. Writing-table, veneered with amboyna and other woods, and parcel gilt. Made by William Jamar, 'French cabinet-maker' of 29, Wardour Street, c. 1815–20. *Length, 4 ft 2 in.*

Fig. 180. Rosewood writing-table, on scrolled legs, headed by lion masks. c. 1810. *Height, 2 ft 5 in.; length, 5 ft.*

Fig. 181. Rosewood writing-table, with bronzed lion-monopodia supports, carved and parcel gilt, and shaped platform base. In the style of George Smith, c. 1810. Length, 5 ft 6 in.

Fig. 182. Rosewood writing-table, or bonheur-du-jour, with gilt enrichments; supported on 'bamboo'-ringed legs. The folding top rests on lopers. The shelved superstructure, above a base of two small drawers, is of brass. Stamped 'E. Butler'. c. 1805.

Fig. 183. Mahogany secretaire cabinet, or bookcase, with glazed upper stage; the cornice surmounted by a carved and gilt eagle and two flammate urns. c. 1800.

Bookcases and Bookshelves

THERE are references to increased demand for bookcases in the early nineteenth century, and to their manufacture by certain cabinet-makers[1] (who 'felt an interest in the increase of books') as 'the leading articles of employ'. The bookcase in two stages, as the secretaire, remained essentially the same (Figs. 183–8). An interesting variant in the Royal Collection has an advanced lower stage surmounted by a white marble slab, and this feature and the quality of the ormolu mounts applied to the frieze and pilasters give it a French air (Fig. 8). In many cases, the bookcase was subjected in its proportions and decorations to Greek canons, and is crowned by a 'Greek' pediment and antefixae.

The bookcase designed by Thomas Hope and formerly at Deepdene (Fig. 18) is an instance of Egyptian massiveness. Each of the cupboard doors of the upper stage is glazed with a single sheet of glass and divided by pilasters headed by Egyptian sphinx-heads, while the projecting base of the upper stage is supported by four lion monopodia. A bookcase of mahogany inlaid with ebony, also in two stages, which was made by George Oakley in 1810 for Papworth Hall, is described by its maker as a 'mahogany winged library case in the Grecian style, the doors fitted with brass trellis wire and quilled silk curtains with best locks and keys'. At either end of the slightly projecting wings are antefixae, and the recessed centre is covered by a small pediment, to which is applied a small-scale enrichment in gilt brass.[2] Dwarf bookcases and cabinets (Figs. 189–94), movable bookstands, chiffoniers and revolving bookcases supplemented, and to some extent ousted, the two-storied type.

Bookcases were affected in their proportions by what George Smith terms the 'lowness adopted in the present design' in order to leave the walls free for paintings.[3] He illustrates dwarf bookcases, one consisting of two pedestal ends and three low compartments, in which the centre is occupied by small books. Such dwarf bookcases were usually made in pairs, and in some instances were surmounted by a marble slab. The doors were glazed or protected by a trellis or mesh of brass wire. Dwarf bookcases were designed for the piers between the windows in the golden drawing-room at Carlton House. Each was surmounted by a marble slab, and fitted with 'angle pillars of palm trees in ormolu'.[4] A feature of bookcases, and cupboards,

[1] Sheraton, *Cabinet Dictionary* (1803), pp. 70–1.
[2] See 'Records of Furniture Makers'.
[3] *Household Furniture* (1808), p. 10.
[4] Pyne, *Royal Residences* (1819), Vol. III, p. 58.

Fig. 184. Mahogany secretaire cabinet, or bookcase, with mouldings and decorative inlaid stringing lines of brass; the upper stage surmounted by a lunette-shaped pediment. c. 1800–5.
Fig. 185. Detail of Fig. 184.

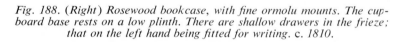

Fig. 186. (Above, left) Secretaire cabinet of mahogany, veneered with zebra wood; the pilasters on the lower stage mounted with Egyptian heads and feet of ormolu. The water-colour drawings in the glazed upper stage are signed 'J. Baynes, 1808'. Height, 5 ft 2½ in.; width, 2 ft 6¾ in.

Fig. 187. (Above, centre) Rosewood secretaire, surmounted by two tiers of brass shelves and mounted with gilt brass. The fall front drawer encloses an interior fitted with pigeon holes and three small drawers. By John McLean, c. 1810. Height, 4 ft 9¾ in.; width, 3 ft ½ in.

Fig. 188. (Right) Rosewood bookcase, with fine ormolu mounts. The cupboard base rests on a low plinth. There are shallow drawers in the frieze; that on the left hand being fitted for writing. c. 1810.

Fig. 189. (Left) Maplewood bookcase, inlaid with ebony; the marble top fitted with a brass gallery. c. 1800.

Fig. 190. (Below) Mahogany dwarf bookcase. c. 1810. Height, 2 ft 11½ in.; length, 4 ft 2½ in.

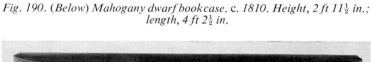

Fig. 191. Rosewood bookcase (one of a pair), with colonnettes of gilt wood, resting on a plinth decorated in imitation of porphyry. c. 1810. Height, 3 ft 2½ in.; length, 5 ft.

Fig. 192. Mahogany bookcase, with gilt lion monopodia, surmounted by a marble slab. c. 1810.

Fig. 193. Low bookcase, veneered with zebra wood, divided by reeded pilasters headed by brass lion masks. c. 1810. Height, 3 ft; length, 5 ft 6½ in.

Fig. 194. Rosewood cabinet-writing table, with decorative brass inlay and gallery. c. 1815.

Fig. 195. Mahogany cupboard, with shelved superstructure bearing a brass gallery; the cupboard doors fitted with wire trellis.

is the open shelved structure which often surmounts them (Fig. 195).

Many low and light bookcases were designed 'calculated to contain all the books that may be desired for a sitting-room without reference to the library'.[1] The type with receding shelves (Fig. 196) and fitted with castors appears in Gillow's Cost books in 1799 as a 'moving library', and this term also appears in the *Cabinet Dictionary*.[2]

A novelty was the circular bookcase or bookstand in which shelves revolve round a central column (Figs. 197 and 198). A patent was taken out in July, 1808 by Benjamin Crosby for 'a machine or stand for books, which may be made either circular, square or any other convenient shape, and which may be turned or moved at pleasure; with cases to receive books'. It is composed of a central shaft or column and fixed shelves at suitable distances above each other containing each a roller or cylinder and screwed to the shaft. A bookshelf is fixed to each cylinder. Each bookshelf is divided into compartments by cross pieces, the interstices being filled up with 'labels and popular books, or in any other ornamental way'.

This type is illustrated in Ackermann's *Repository of Arts* for March, 1810 as an 'ingenious contrivance' (Fig. 199). The projector, according to the note accompanying the plate, 'seems to have had in recollection the conveniences afforded by the set of circular and movable tables formerly known by the appellation of dumb waiters'. A cylindrical pedestal, formed of two shelves as a base, supports the upper and movable part, which consists of shelves progressively diminishing in diameter.

'Each shelf is furnished with a corresponding shelf at a distance above it, and the two shelves thus situated are moved horizontally about an upright centre which passes through the whole machine.' The pedestal is furnished with substantial feet and rollers, so that the piece can be wheeled to different parts of a room, or from one room to another. 'This bookcase', the note continues, 'appears to afford some valuable conveniences, as, for instance, it may be placed in a recess, or in a corner of a room in which from local circumstances it might be inconvenient or impossible to dispose the same number of books.' In some cases, dummy books divide the shelves, and in the design there is a turned wooden urn finial. 'The machine' was 'manufactured by permission' by Morgan and Sanders and was to be seen in their showrooms in Catherine Street.

LIBRARY STEPS

Library steps, which are defined in the *Cabinet Dictionary* as steps placed 'in a library, for the use of raising a person so as to reach at any book', were an essential part of the furniture of large libraries, and were often contrived to fold up into the upper part of a stool or table. Library steps were described in a survey of Alnwick in 1785, where one of a pair of tables was 'by an ingenious device opened and forms a pair of commodious steps for reaching any of the Books from the higher shelves'.

[1] Ackermann's *Repository of Arts*, 1823.
[2] 'The tea-room or breakfast-room may abound with . . . moving libraries' — p. 219.

Fig. 196. Mahogany bookcase, shelved on either side. c. *1800.*

Fig. 197. Mahogany revolving bookshelves, on a table stand. c. *1800.*

Fig. 198. (Left) Rosewood revolving bookshelves, on a table stand; the stand, on three central column supports and triangular platform base, with carved and gilt enrichments. c. *1810.*

Fig. 199. (Above) Design for a 'Circular Bookcase', from Ackermann's Repository of Arts, *March, 1810. Recommended for use on 'occasions of literary research and reference'.*

The two examples of library steps illustrated in the *Appendix* to Sheraton's *Drawing Book* were, he writes, taken 'from steps made by Mr Campbell, upholsterer to the Prince of Wales', and were first made for George III. In one design 'the table when enclosed, serves as a library table and has a rising flap, supported by a base, to write on'. In the second, and simple design, the upper flight of steps folds down upon the under flight, and both rise up and slide into the frieze, which is afterwards closed by a flap, which has the appearance of a drawer front. The resting post at the top also folds down to the side of the steps.

In 1811, Morgan and Sanders showed a design in Ackermann's *Repository of Arts*, for a metamorphic library chair, in which 'an elegant and comfortable library chair' is combined with a set of steps. As may be seen from the illustration of the contrivance in the Library of Trinity College, Oxford, the chair is converted into steps by turning the back of the chair downwards. It 'corresponds so closely with the design as to leave no doubt of its origin. After one hundred and twenty years it still justifies the makers' claim that it is firm, safe and solid as a rock' (Figs. 200 and 201).[1]

[1] Described and illustrated, *Country Life*, September 20, 1930.

Figs. 200 and 201. Mahogany library chair and steps combined. 'The Patent Metamorphic Library Chair', made by Morgan and Sanders and described in Ackermann's Repository of Arts *for 1811 as 'a novel and useful article'.*

Sideboards, Dining and Drinking Accessories

THE sideboard table without drawers flanked by separate pedestals[1] carrying vases or knife boxes, a development of the type designed by Robert Adam, continued to be made. In the inventory of furniture at Papworth Hall (in 1810) there is an entry of a 'capital mahogany sideboard supported on a stand, reeded legs and carved and bronzed paw feet with antique bronze heads', and pedestals to match.[2]

Many tables, dating from the second decade of the century, are supported on lion monopodia, chimeras or gryphons (Figs. 202 and 203). Some later specimens, influenced by French models in the style of Louis XIV, have scrolled console supports.

The sideboard fitted with pedestal cupboards developed into a massive piece of furniture with a considerable storage-capacity[3] (Figs. 205 and 206). Such pedestals, prolonged almost to the floor and often rising above the level of the centre, were sometimes fitted with a drawer at the top. A rosewood sideboard of about 1815–20, in the Victoria and Albert Museum, shows the late features of projecting central shelf with a high scrolled back-piece (replacing the brass gallery), flanked by two tapering pedestals, each fitted with two drawers. Each pedestal supports a tapering rectangular knife-box with a hinged lid and feet in the form of brass balls (Fig. 207). The form of pedestals and boxes is perhaps Egyptian in origin. Fig. 208 shows an unusual piece designed to fit the angle of a room.

DINING AND DRINKING ACCESSORIES (WINE TABLES, DUMB WAITERS)

As prolonged drinking after dinner was still a polite custom, specialised wine or 'social' tables were produced in the second half of the eighteenth century. A gentleman's social table, figured in the *Cabinet Makers' London Book of Prices* for 1793, shows a kidney-shaped table for the sitters, combined with a smaller table, in which the drum consists of a cylinder of tin or copper, and 'a mahogany top fitted into the cylinder, and cut to receive five tin bottle-cases'. A horseshoe-shaped drinking table, fitted with two japanned ice-pails, is figured in Gillow's Cost books for July, 1801, where it is described as a 'social table'.[4] In an example from the London Museum, the bottles were con-

---

[1] Pedestals were 'designed for holding plates for dinner' and contained racks and a heater, according to Sheraton, *Cabinet Dictionary* (1803). In Smith's *Household Furniture* (1808), one pedestal is fitted as a plate-warmer, while the other contains a tray capable of holding six or eight bottles.

[2] MS. inventory of furniture supplied by Oakley for Papworth Hall.

[3] A sideboard formerly in Nelson's cabin in the *Victory*, and dating from about 1800, is of this type, having deep pedestal ends, each fitted with a drawer and a cupboard, a projecting centre, and panelled back-piece, rising above the top of the sideboard. Exhibited on loan in the forecabin of the *Victory*, 1928.

[4] An early reference to a specialised drinking table is at Howth Castle (1746–52), where a 'round mahogany drinking-table appears in the dining parlour' — Ball, *The House of Howth*, p. 164.

Fig. 202. *Mahogany sideboard table, supported on lion monopodia, fitted with a brass gallery. (The cellaret of earlier date.) c. 1810.*

Fig. 203. *Mahogany sideboard table, supported on carved chimeras, with carved bronzed enrichments and gallery. c. 1815. Height, 4 ft 4½ in.; length, 7 ft 10½ in.*

Fig. 204. Carved mahogany sideboard, intended for service of wines; of unusual type (in form reminiscent of a cassone). The recessed centre contains a cupboard enclosed by doors with provision for sets of glasses and decanters; at the ends are lead-lined cellarettes. c. 1805. Length, 6 ft 2 in.

Fig. 205. Mahogany pedestal sideboard, with shaped front, concave in the centre. c. 1810. [According to Sheraton in the Drawing Book (1791–4) '. . . the hollow front will sometimes secure the butler from the jostles of the other servants'.] Height, 3 ft 3 in.; length, 7 ft.

Fig. 206. Mahogany pedestal sideboard, inlaid with stringing lines. c. 1810. Height, 5 ft; length, 8 ft 7½ in.

Fig. 207. (Below, left) Rosewood pedestal sideboard, decorated with brass inlay. The form of the pedestals, and the surmounting knife boxes, is distinctive, and the scrolled outline of the back a late feature. c. 1815–20.

Fig. 208. (Below) Mahogany sideboard, shaped to fit an angle, and supported by lion monopodia. c. 1800.

tained in two metal coasters, hinged to a brass rod. In some examples, adjustable circular fans are fitted to the table to serve as fire-screens.

The dumb waiter of the Regency period, defined in the *Cabinet Dictionary* (1803) as a 'useful piece of furniture, to serve in some respects the place of a waiter', commonly departs from the earlier patterns in the form of its tripod (Fig. 209). 'There are different kinds of these waiters', adds Sheraton, 'but they are all made of mahogany, and are intended for the use of the dining parlour, on which to place glasses of wine, and plates, both clean, and such as have been used.'

PLATE AND CUTLERY STANDS (CANTERBURIES)

Among the convenient accessories introduced into the dining-room in the late eighteenth century were stands for carrying plates, and larger stands partitioned into spaces for cutlery and plates (Figs. 210 and 211). Sheraton defines these 'supper Canterburies' as 'made to stand by a table at supper, with a circular end, and three partitions cross wise, to hold knives, forks, and plates, at that end, which is made circular on purpose',[1] and illustrates two designs, one having a circular top and platform below fitted with small divisions; the other having a tray top, with a platform divided into partitions for knives, forks, etc. They have spindle galleries and are supported on turned legs of circular section. Smaller Canterburies were sometimes made in pairs, one for plates (with circular top), the other for cutlery (with tray top). The vogue for this article of furniture was not continued into Victorian times.

[1] Op. cit., p. 127.

Fig. 209. Mahogany dumb waiter, inlaid with ebony; the lowest tier fitted with candle stands, the uppermost with hinged flaps. c. 1810. Height, 4 ft 4½ in.

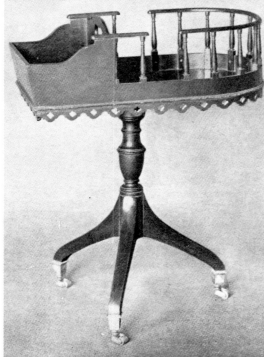

Fig. 210. Mahogany plate stand or 'Canterbury'. c. 1795. Height, 2 ft 3½ in.

Fig. 211. Mahogany plate stand or 'Canterbury', on turned legs; the top divided with a partition for plates and partitions for cutlery. c. 1810.

Pedestals, The What-not, Music Canterburies and Fire-screens

PEDESTALS for lamps, candelabra, vases or busts were characteristic of the period, and the form was adapted for the display of classical ornament. In George Smith's *Household Furniture* (1808), they are recommended for a number of purposes and situations: 'In galleries for pictures or antiquities these supports are appropriate for Busts and Statues; they are equally useful in halls and on staircases, and need not be rejected in drawing-rooms.' In the latter place, they served to carry vases or figures bearing branches for lights.

The four pedestals of gilt wood (Fig. 212), are among those made for the Prince Regent in 1811 by Tatham & Co. They are based on the Roman type of candelabrum.[1] They figure in Pyne's view of the Crimson Drawing Room at Carlton House.[2]

THE WHAT-NOT

The what-not, defined in the *New English Dictionary* as 'an open stand with shelves one above another for keeping or displaying various objects, as ornaments, curiosities, books, papers, etc', is not illustrated in trade-catalogues of the late eighteenth century, but is mentioned in the year 1808.[3] An early evidence of this type is the rosewood example fitted with shelves, and mounted with ormolu (Fig. 213). In some cases

[1] There exists in the Naples Museum a bronze found at Pompeii with the *motif* of three cranes standing back to back upon a triangular base.

[2] *Royal Residences* (1819).

[3] 'The old chairs, tables, what-nots and sofas' — Sarah, Lady Lyttleton, *Correspondence* (1808) (ed. 1902), p. 54.

Fig. 212. Carved and gilt pedestal (one of a set of four 'very large elegant tripods superbly carved and double gilt'), made for Carlton House in 1811 by Tatham, Bailey & Saunders at a cost of £143 each. Height (with candelabrum), 8 ft 2 in.

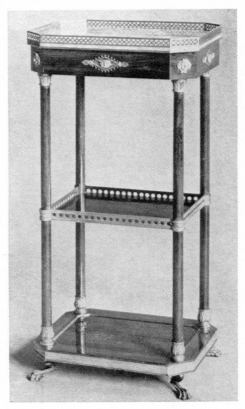

Fig. 213. Rosewood what-not (one of a pair), mounted with ormolu. c. 1800.

Fig. 214. Stand or what-not (one of a pair), of black painted wood with white inlaid stringing lines, and with rings gilt; the lower part fitted with two drawers, the top with a marble slab and brass gallery. c. 1800.

Fig. 215. Rosewood music stand, with wire trellis sides. c. 1815. Height, 2 ft 3½ in.; width, 2 ft.

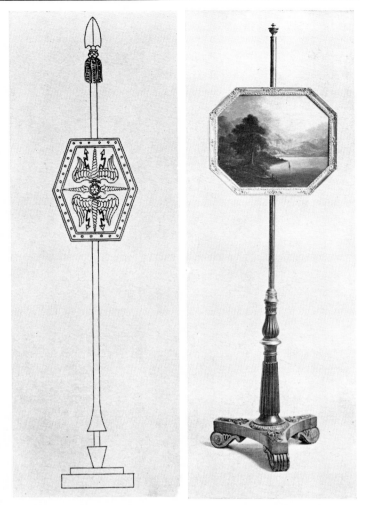

the base contained a shallow drawer, or drawers (Fig. 214).

Stands to hold music and portfolios for the numerous engravings published at this time also became recognised as necessary pieces of furniture.

MUSIC CANTERBURIES

Under this term music stands are defined by Sheraton in his *Cabinet Dictionary* as made 'with two or three hollow topped partitions, framed in light slips of mahogany, about three inches apart from each other, and about 8 inches deep', resting on legs fitted with casters and 'adapted to run in under a piano-forte'. In the rosewood canterbury (Fig. 215), with sides fitted with wire trellis-work, to hold the bound music books and portfolios, there is a drawer beneath designed to contain unbound music.

FIRE-SCREENS

The fire-screen was an article of general use, and 'admitted of every species of decoration according to the character of the room'.[1] Types of screen in production at the beginning of the nineteenth century include the 'tripod' fire-screen, or pole screen, a light movable object, designed to shield a person's face from the fire; the horse (cheval) or 'safe' fire-screen, which stood by the hearth; the 'folding and sliding' screen — a development of the cheval screen, constructed with 'frames to slide out on the sides'[2] or with frame to draw upwards; and small table fire-screens.

From about 1815 the banner-screen, in which an unframed piece of fabric hung from a transverse rod, became popular (Fig. 62).

Hope's design for a pole-screen (Fig. 216) is interesting because of its classical impress. (A pair of rosewood pole-screens with carved and gilt enrichments executed from his design were formerly at Deepdene. The brass poles are shaped as lances, and the panels as Grecian shields, carved with classical thunderbolts.)

A distinctive feature of numerous pole-screens of this period is the solid base or block (circular or triangular in shape) (Fig. 217), upon which the pole rests. The tripod base persists, however, often in the form of animal supports (Fig. 218). The framed panels were usually painted or worked in a design such as 'the taste of the amateur may suggest'.[3]

[1] and [2] Smith, op. cit.
[3] Ackermann's *Repository of Arts*, 1815.

Fig. 216. Design for a pole-screen, from Hope's Household Furniture *(1807), Plate 18, No. 2.*

Fig. 217. Mahogany pole-screen, on flat triangular base; framing a landscape in an octagonal frame. c. 1825.

Fig. 218. Rosewood parcel gilt pole-screen; the panel painted with arabesques in water-colour by L. A. Delabrière (a French artist who painted the walls of the boudoir at Southill). Probably designed by Henry Holland. c. 1805.

Commodes and Chiffoniers

IT proved impossible to translate the eighteenth-century commode, which depended so largely upon its subtlety of shaping and its surface decoration of marquetry and painting, into the new classical idiom. Thomas Hope gives no design for the commode, for which no classical precedent existed. Commodes 'intended for the drawing-rooms and also for living-rooms, [having] therefore doors to screen or secure such articles as may be placed in them' are, however, illustrated in George Smith's *Household Furniture* (1808), and described as being made of 'rosewood, satinwood, or in gold on a white ground, or japanned in imitation of the finer woods', and as fitted with marble or marbled tops (Fig. 29). They are straight-fronted and of massive, box-like form, and are distinct from those commodes (and related pier-tables), influenced by French models (the Louis XVI *commodes ouvertes*), which were fashionable about the turn of the century.

Later Regency commodes, in the French Empire manner, are of heavy architectural character. They are supported on a low plinth, and the cupboard doors are often flanked by columns of wood or marble. Metal grille doors are a decorative feature of commodes, dwarf cupboards and cabinets.

The place of the commode was taken by a low shelved cupboard, called a chiffonier, which, as its name indicates, was of French introduction, and appears in French inventories about the middle of the eighteenth century. As described by Havard,[1] the chiffonier contained many drawers in which papers, jewels and '*chiffons*' could be stored. The '*chiffonnière*' was in effect a

[1] *Dictionnaire de l'ameublement*, Vol. I, p. 806.

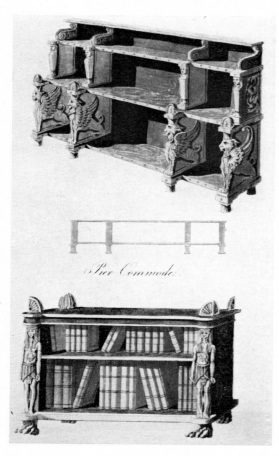

Fig. 219. Designs for 'Chiffonier' and 'Pier Commode', dated 1804, from George Smith's Household Furniture (1808), Plate 115.

Fig. 220. Rosewood cabinet or commode-chiffonier (one of a pair), with wire trellis doors. c. 1820. Height (to top of cabinet), 3 ft; height of superstructure, 1 ft 4½ in.; width, 3 ft.

tall, relatively narrow commode chest of drawers. '*Chiffonnières*' were to be distinguished from '*commodes*', but were comparable with them. (The name appears at an early date in England in Thomas Chippendale's bills for furniture supplied to Sir Edward Knatchbull for Mersham Hatch: 'a neat shiffeneer writing table japaned green and gold, with a drawer and cut bottles'. This, however, was likely to have been an English version of the '*table en chiffonnière*', a small table containing a single drawer, which was an entirely separate article of furniture.) Chiffoniers are illustrated by George Smith in the form of low, open and shelved cupboards (Fig. 219). In appearance they closely resemble low bookcases and served much the same purpose. Smith observes: 'in almost every apartment of a house these articles will be found useful . . . chiefly for such books as are in constant use, or not of sufficient consequence for the library; on the same account they become extremely serviceable in libraries for the reception of books taken for present reading . . . the most simple are manufactured in plain mahogany, or japanned in imitation of various woods; the more elegant in mahogany with decoration in imitation of bronze metal.'[1]

Chiffoniers are among those 'articles of the newest fashion' which Robert Southey, in 1807, suggests 'will soon be thought indispensably necessary in every well furnished house'.[2] He asks: '*Commodes, Console-tables* . . . and *Chiffoniers;* — what are all these?' and finds 'no person in the house' to give him an answer[3] (Figs. 195 and 220).

Chiffoniers were purposed to display china as well as books, and were made in a variety of patterns. Many specimens were provided with a superstructure of shelves, with scrolled supports. In some cases an enclosed central portion, with grille doors, was flanked by open sides. The Nicholsons, in their *Practical Cabinet Maker* (1826–7) do not differentiate between the commode and the chiffonier.

---

[1] In 1805, however, Samuel Beckwith supplied Windsor Castle with two satinwood 'chiffoniers ornamented with black lines, inlaid, with two drawers each, brass rims round tops and furniture, with locks casters and frames varnished' — Bill for furniture for the drawing-room, Windsor Castle, Lord Chamberlain's Office, P.R.O.

[2] *Letters from England: by Don Manuel Alvarez Espirella. Translated from the Spanish* (1807). The text was written by Southey between 1803–7 and refers to a visit of 1802–3.

[3] The term appears in print at this time: C. K. Sharpe, *Letters* (1806), refers to 'a small, helpless family of chiffoniers, writing tables and footstools'.

Mirrors

LARGE mirrors, hung on the walls to produce 'an endless vista', were considered a necessary part of English luxury.[1] Immense looking-glasses with gilt frames (according to Papworth's edition of the *Decorative Part of Civil Architecture*) superseded the carved and painted superstructure of the fireplace, and the chimney-piece was reduced from its late magnificence 'to the duty of supporting clocks, girandoles, vases and bijoutry'. In a house in Sussex described in the *New Vitruvius*

Britannicus (1802) living-rooms of very moderate dimensions were so disposed that when the large folding doors were open they made one apartment and the glasses over the chimney-pieces of the two extreme rooms gave the appearance of an 'endless suite'.[2]

[1] Fückler-Muskau, *Tour in Germany, Holland and England* (1826), Vol. III, p. 102.
[2] Vol. I, p. 14.

Fig. 221. From E. W. Brayley's Illustrations of Her Majesty's Palace at Brighton; formerly the Pavilion (*1838*), Plate XIX—*the 'Saloon, in its present state'.*

Fig. 222. Chimney mirror, in gilt frame; the frieze mounted with small convex mirrors and decorated with classical figures in low relief. c. 1800.

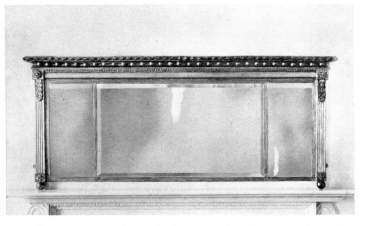

Fig. 223. Chimney mirror, in gilt frame; the bevelled plates divided by reeded mouldings; the cavetto frieze with small gilt balls. c. 1805.

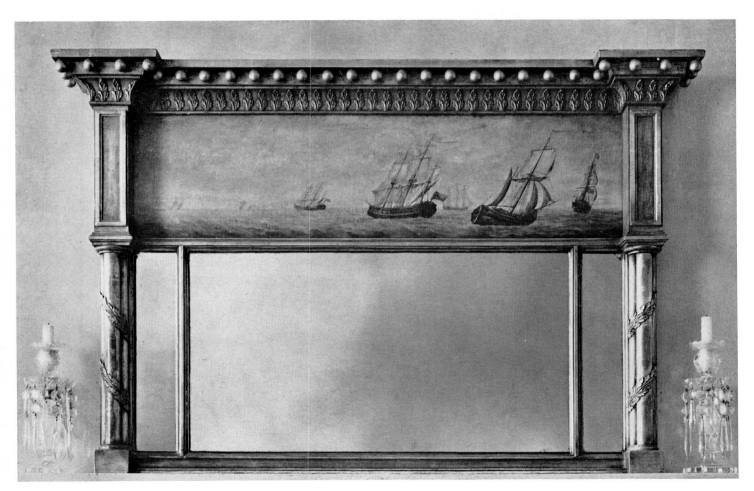

Fig. 224. Gilt chimney mirror, framing in the upper part a painting of ships at sea. c. 1805.

The rectangular pier- and chimney-glasses were often of great size during the last years of the eighteenth and the early nineteenth centuries. In the saloon at the Prince of Wales's Pavilion at Brighton a large looking-glass, thirteen feet high, and eight feet wide, was fixed over the chimney-piece[1] (Fig. 221), and George Smith recommends that chimney- and pier-glasses should not have any ornament or head-pieces, but be 'carried quite to the cornice of the room'.[2] The frames were comparatively narrow, and often reeded. Heavier and more elaborate frames, with foliate ornament, returned to favour before the end of the first quarter of the century.

During the eighteenth century, and especially during the later years, it was customary to have a glass above the chimney-shelf extending nearly its length. Chimney-glasses of the earlier Regency period were low and broad and flanked by pilasters or

[1] E. W. Brayley, *Illustrations of Her Majesty's Palace at Brighton* (1838), p. 10.
[2] *Household Furniture* (1808), p. 22.

Fig. 225. Mirror, in carved and gilt frame, surmounted by a Greek pediment, with acroters. c. 1810.

Fig. 226. Convex mirror, in gilt wood frame. c. 1805.

attached columns. Commonly, they were surmounted by a cornice with hollow (cavetto) moulding in which rows of balls were set and the glass was divided into three sections (Figs. 33, 222–4). An upper panel, or frieze, was sometimes decorated in bas-relief, or by back painting, with *verre églomisé*, or a picture.

A number of small upright gilt mirrors of architectural character and of much the same type were also made (Fig. 225).

Convex mirrors, which 'strengthen the colour and take off the coarseness of objects by contracting them', were, by 1803, 'universally in fashion'; 'the perspective of the room in which they are suspended', observes Sheraton, 'presents itself on the surface of the mirror, and produces an agreeable effect'.[1] They were made in various dimensions from about a foot in diameter to three feet, the plate enclosed in a gilt frame fitted

often with candle branches on either side and surmounted by an eagle displayed, above the cresting of acanthus foliage (Fig. 226). There was normally an ebonised fillet next the glass, a cavetto and outer band usually reeded and crossed at intervals by ribands. In the mirror from the Merchant Taylors' Hall, the finial is formed by the crest of the Company, 'a lamb silver in beams gold', resting upon entwined cornucopiae. The slightly concave border of the frame is enriched with trellis-work and in place of the usual sconce arms are female terms holding torches (Plate III). In late examples the small balls applied to the deep cavetto moulding of the frame are more widely spaced, and the acanthus carving at cresting and base (which is also a feature of most frames) is bolder and coarser in execution. Convex mirrors of this form remained in fashion until about 1830.

[1] *Cabinet Dictionary* (1803), p. 271.

III. Convex mirror, in gilt wood frame.

Lighting Fittings

AFTER the economical illumination of the eighteenth century, the lighting of the Regency period was recognised as an advance in comfort. The new demand for adequate lighting was reinforced by the knowledge that the glass and metal which formed the chandeliers and many of the candelabra were the products of English industries which deserved to be encouraged.

The chief lighting fitting was the chandelier suspended from the ceiling. According to a writer in the *Morning Post* (1808) 'every other light, except that produced by cut-glass chandeliers is dispensed with, the candelabra and girandole being found to produce only a local light'. During the last decade of the eighteenth century, the chandelier was 'conceived as a solid'[1]

and some examples were designed after a classical vase form. In the Regency period, the principle of design was 'a set of cylinders enclosing one another, and superimposed one upon another'. Each cylinder was composed of pendant 'fingers' of glass. An example of this treatment is the design made in 1811 for the Emperor of China by Perry & Parker.[2] In another pattern a glass canopy (formed of drops) descends to a rim of brass or bronze, from which lines of drops are caught up into a bowl (Fig. 227). The angularity of many designs of this period is noted by Alison,[3] who describes the 'form of the Prism, one

[1] W. A. Thorpe, *English and Greek Glass*, Vol. I, p. 317.
[2] See 'Records of Furniture Makers'.
[3] *Essays on Taste* (1790), p. 366.

Fig. 227. Chandelier, of metal and cut glass. c. 1815.

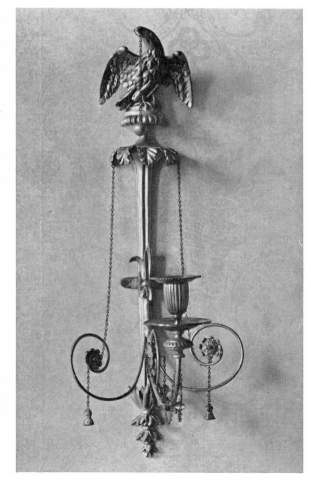

Fig. 228. Carved and gilt wall-light for one candle. c 1805.
Height, 1 ft 11½ in.

Fig. 229. Candelabrum, of gilt brass, hung with cut glass.

Fig. 230. Candlestick, with cut glass drum and gilt brass stem, fitted with a bell-shaped ground glass shade painted in the Chinese taste. c. 1820. Height, 1 ft 3¼ in.; diameter of top, 6¾ in.

of the most angular of all forms', as obtaining everywhere, 'the Festoons even are angular; and instead of any winding or waving Line, the whole surface is broken into a thousand little Triangles'.

The account books of Messrs. Perry contained evidence of a wide sale of English chandeliers abroad; Lord Elgin, in 1799, presented a chandelier to the Grand Seigneur, who was captivated with it, 'declaring it to be the most superb thing he ever saw and proposing to build a room on purpose for it.'[1]

The great lustres are overpowering accessories in the views of Carlton House in Pyne's *Royal Residences*. These lustres, built of ormolu hung with pendants and festoons of faceted glass, are described in detail in the Carlton House accounts. Their cost was surprisingly high; in 1808 a 'magnificent fifty-six light lustre was made for the Great Drawing-room for a thousand guineas, designed to represent a fountain falling into a large reservoir'. A lustre of glass and ormolu at Carlton House is described as looking like a shower of diamonds. Perry & Parker (and, subsequently, Perry & Co.) continued to provide a succession of lighting fittings displaying the Chinese, Greek and Gothic styles until Carlton House was dismantled in 1826. The immense size and cost of the lustres at Carlton House and at the Brighton Pavilion is the subject of comments in letters and journals.

Rooms were also lighted by girandoles or wall-lights (Fig. 228), and by candelabra set upon the chimney-piece or upon pedestals. These pedestals for lamps and candelabra were characteristic of the robust and Roman rendering of the classic. Figures carrying lights were, as in France, in fashion, and Sheraton, in 1803, mentions the fact that figure lights have been a recent introduction.[2,3]

The concealment of lights in semi-transparent alabaster vases was borrowed from France, where Madame Recamier's bedroom, when Samuel Rogers saw it in 1802, was 'lighted with aromatic lamps and alabaster vases'. This device is described by Warner in the same year as existing in the dining-room at Newby, in Yorkshire, where the room was lighted by several large 'transparent alabaster vases standing upon pedestals intended to receive candles'. The light of candles concealed within an alabaster vase must have been, as it is described, 'dim and religious'.[4]

Glass candlesticks and candelabra with one or more lights continued to be made with bases of varied materials (Fig. 229). The heavy drum of marble, ormolu, earthenware, or coloured glass, gave stability to the candelabrum. A number of candlesticks fitted with large glass shades, painted and ground, were made in the early nineteenth century (Figs. 230 and 231), but, owing to the fragility of glass, few have survived.

[1] *Letters of Mary Nisbet, Countess of Elgin* (1926), p. 54.
[2] *Correspondence of Sarah, Lady Lyttleton*, p. 104.
[3] *Cabinet Dictionary* (1803), p. 261.
[4] R. Warner, *Tour through the Northern Counties* (1802), p. 137.

Fig. 231. Sheffield plate candlestick, with painted glass shade. c. 1820.

Fig. 232. Bronze standing lamp for three burners, with gilt enrichments. In the style of George Smith, c. 1810. Height, 6 ft 8 in.

LAMPS

Lamps (vessels in which oil is burnt with a wick) were of either standard or hanging form, and were adapted also for use as wall-lights (Figs. 232–4). An improvement adopted in England about 1786[1] was the Argand lamp, named after its Swiss inventor, who perfected his invention between 1780 and 1783. A large number of Argand patent lamps were made by Matthew Boulton in his Soho works, near Birmingham, and Wedgwood, in 1787, advertises 'lamps of two colours, adapted to Argand's patent lamp, the brilliant light of which being thrown on the bas-reliefs, has a singular and beautiful effect'. The burner was made up of two concentric tubes carrying the wick between them, a system which allowed a double current of air, and thus more perfect combustion. Their advantage lies in a wick which burns around a tube fixed within a glass funnel higher than the flame with an air current beneath to prevent flickering and smoke. The container for the oil was, in the case of colza, a heavy oil, placed at a higher level than the burner (or burners) so that the oil descended by gravitation.

Hanging lamps of metal were designed after antique Roman models, with spreading, boat-shaped arms connected with an urn-shaped container (usually by about 1810, of globular, Roman form) for heavy oil placed at a higher level (Figs. 235

[1] When Sophie von La Roche relates: 'we finished the evening at tea investigating Argand lamps of all descriptions' — *Sophie in London, 1786* (1933).

Fig. 233. Bronze hanging lamp for two burners, with gilt enrichments. c. 1810. Length, 1 ft 10 in.

Fig. 234. Hanging lamp for one burner, suspended from a carved and gilt eagle. c. 1805.

and 236). The burner was protected by an upright glass shade or globe. In several cases the ornament applied to the bronzed frame was gilt brass. It was noted in the account books of the firm of Perry between 1812 and 1820 that burners and chains were often of French make.

Lamps were also placed on stands at a convenient height, and stands or pedestals are figured in George Smith's *Household Furniture* (1808), where it is recommended that these should be placed in the angles of drawing-rooms, or 'by the sides of large sofas, in continuation throughout the length of the room'.

In 1802 the younger Thomas Chippendale supplied Sir Richard Colt Hoare at Stourhead with 'a rich candelabrum for four lights . . . with a variety of carved ornamental work with goats' heads and lions' feet, the pillars reeded and finished in burnished gold'. Examples of similar monumental pieces exist at Castle Coole, and in the hall of Syon House (Fig. 237).

Gas as a new and revolutionary illuminant was introduced and was admired as a novelty at Lambton Hall in 1821 by Sidney Smith, who wrote that 'the splendour and glory of Lambton make all other houses mean. It is pitiful', he adds, 'to submit to a farthing candle-existence when Science puts such intense gratification within your reach. Dear Lady, spend all your fortune on a gas apparatus'.

Fig. 235. Bronze hanging lamp for four burners. c. 1815. Height, 4 ft 7 in.

Fig. 236. Bronze hanging lamp, with gilt enrichments; engraved with maker's name, James Delville, and dated 1817.

Fig. 237. Gilt metal standard lamp (one of a set), resting on a mahogany and gilt pedestal; the four burners fed from the urn-shaped container on top. c. 1800. Height, 8 ft 10 in.

Clock and Pianoforte Cases

THE long-case clock is described by Sheraton in his *Cabinet Dictionary* (1803) as almost obsolete in London, and no examples are illustrated by him in this work.

The leading English clockmakers were influenced by the competition of the French, and a German visitor to London[1] in 1786 describes the works of Vulliamy, the Court clockmaker, as 'of exquisite beauty and perfection'. Benjamin Vulliamy was frequently in attendance upon George III at Kew, and his son, Benjamin Lewis Vulliamy (1780–1854), a man of informed taste, and a clockmaker who introduced several improvements in horology, assisted in the alterations made by the Prince of Wales at Carlton House. In a clock made by him for the Brighton Pavilion, about 1820, the movement is fitted into a Chinese vase of the K'ang Hsi period, and surrounded by sprays of sunflowers in ormolu and flanked by kylins of the Ch'ien Lung period.

The designers of cases of bracket clocks assimilated the *motifs* of the day, and showed the same tendency to simplification. In the early nineteenth century the tops of clocks were often lancet-shaped (Fig. 238). Veneers of mahogany, ebony and rosewood were chiefly employed for the case, sometimes enriched by brass lines.

ACT OF PARLIAMENT CLOCKS

Large-faced wall clocks having a short case were hung in public rooms and taverns from the mid-eighteenth century, and to these the name 'Act of Parliament clocks' is sometimes given, though it is a misnomer to apply that term to a wall clock carrying a date anterior to the year 1797 when (under William Pitt's administration) an annual tax of five shillings was imposed on all clocks, which reduced the demand by one-half. Tavern-keepers, foreseeing a scarcity of clocks and watches among their public, put up cheaply-made clocks with a large dial and drop case in prominent positions on the walls of their public rooms. The short-lived and unpopular Act was repealed in April, 1798. The Act of Parliament clocks, improvised to meet an emergency, have large wooden dials, usually japanned black, and unglazed (for easy reading), and a trunk of stunted form. The production of mural clocks of this type continued for many years.

[1] Sophie von La Roche (*Sophie in London, 1786* (1933), p. 100) writes: 'it is no prejudice on my part if I state that no Paris invention comes up to those which I saw here, and truly, ideas of practical value cannot be more nobly represented'. The firm of Vulliamy obtained the appointment of clockmakers to the Crown in 1742, and held it for 112 years.

Fig. 238. Bracket clock; the case of mahogany, with Egyptian motifs; the movement by Brockbank & Atkins, London. The supporting wall bracket is not shown. c. 1815.

PIANOFORTE CASES

The first pianos made in England soon after 1760 were the work of a German, Johannes Zumpe, who entered Burkat Shudi's service, and his square pianos soon became the vogue; everyone who considered himself a person of fashion had a pianoforte as a matter of course.[1] In the late years of the century three patents were granted for upright pianofortes: Landreth's (1787), Stodart's (1795), and William Southwell's (1798). Stodart's patent was for an upright pianoforte 'in the form of a bookcase', and Haydn, who visited his shop in Lad Lane, was delighted with its new possibilities. Stodart's grand piano was encased in a rectangular upright cupboard and placed on a stand. The case of an upright piano by Stodart in the Metropolitan Museum, New York, is of mahogany, with the name board in satinwood painted with floral swags. The upper portion is fitted with glass rods backed with white velvet painted with floral pendants and musical instruments. The four-legged stand is inlaid with stringing lines.[2] This pattern began to go out of fashion about the end of the first quarter of the nineteenth century. The patent of William Southwell of Dublin shows a design for a square pianoforte placed on its side on a stand.

An example of his upright square pianofortes has a mahogany case, banded with satinwood and rosewood, and centring in a trophy of musical instruments.[3] The year 1800 saw the invention by two pianoforte-makers simultaneously[4] of an instrument resting 'directly upon the floor, and dispensing with a stand'. Thomas Jefferson, who visited Philadelphia in that year, writes that 'a very ingenious, modest and poor young man has invented one of the prettiest improvements in the pianoforte that I have ever seen, and it has tempted me to engage one for the Montebello. The strings are perpendicular, and he contrives within that height to give his strings the same length as in a grand pianoforte'.[5]

There is only one recorded example of Hawkins's portable grand pianoforte, which is in the possession of Messrs. Broadwood. The case is mahogany, and the pilasters at the angles bear Egyptian heads and finish in brass feet.

[1] R. E. M. Harding, *The History of the Pianoforte*, p. 54.
[2] and [3] Illustrated in Ralph Edwards' *Dictionary of English Furniture* (revised ed. 1954), Vol. II, pp. 377, 378.
[4] Matthias Müller, of Vienna, and Isaac Hawkins, of Philadelphia.
[5] Quoted in E. Singleton, *Furniture of Our Forefathers*, p. 521.

Bedroom Furniture

AN example of a domed state bed of this period is that at Ragley, where the dome is surmounted by antefixae and finishes in a plume of ostrich feathers (Fig. 239); a comparable bed at Wimpole Hall (Fig. 240) was prepared for George IV when Prince of Wales. The familiar types, 'four post' and 'field bed', of the late eighteenth century, were also in use in the early nineteenth century. The 'field bed', named from its tent-like appearance, was lighter than the four-post bed with its cornice and tester, and the curved rods uniting the tops of the posts formed a dome above the curtains. A new pattern, the couch, or canopy or French bed, was copied from French designs, having either a low straight head and backboard, or outward-curving scroll ends. In designs, this simplified structure is surmounted by a curtain supported either by a single pole fixed to the wall, or by a small tester.[1]

[1] George Smith, *Guide* (1828), p. 182.

Fig. 239. Bed, with curtains and valances of painted silk surmounted by the Prince of Wales's plume of feathers. c. 1810.

Fig. 240. A four-post canopied and domed bed; carved and gilt wood. c. 1810.

Fig. 241. Mahogany chest of drawers; bow-fronted, with spiral-twisted colonnettes at the angles. c. 1810. Height, 3 ft 6 in.; length, 3 ft 8 in.

Fig. 242. Grained chest of drawers, with 'bamboo' mouldings. c. 1830.

Fig. 243. Mahogany wardrobe, in the Egyptian taste. c. 1807. Height, 7 ft 9 in.; width, 4 ft 5½ in.

CHESTS OF DRAWERS

The double chest of drawers was less popular during the Regency period, and George Smith describes this article as being made lower than usual, to 'avoid the disagreeable alternative of getting on to chairs to place anything in the upper drawers'.[1] Chests of drawers were usually either straight or bow-fronted. Distinctive features of the last years of the eighteenth and the early nineteenth century are the deep frieze above the top drawer, and the presence of reeded quarter columns, or pilasters, at the front angles. About 1810 spirally twisted colonnettes (Fig. 241) were introduced at the front angles. Sometimes, in late specimens, these members are completely detached, rising from a deep plinth.

Much bedroom furniture was made in a cheap wood, such as beech or deal, painted or grained. Fig. 242 is a pleasing example of such furniture.

WARDROBES

When the tall double chest of drawers went out of fashion, it was superseded by a hanging press or wardrobe,[2] which in large examples consisted of a clothes press and wings. In form, this piece resembled a break-front bookcase, but was made with solid doors, enclosing shelves for clothes; hanging accommodation was in the wings. Later wardrobes often exhibit a considerable variation in height between the different compartments; and some were made with a depressed centre portion. Fig. 243 illustrates a press, without wings, in the Egyptian taste. Dwarf wardrobes also enjoyed some popularity.

[1] *Household Furniture* (1808), p. 24.
[2] A large bedroom in *Northanger Abbey* (1803) was furnished with 'a handsome family bed . . . a bright Bath stove, mahogany wardrobe' (Chapter XXIV).

CHEVAL GLASSES AND DRESSING GLASSES

The 'Psyche', or long glass raised and lowered between its uprights or swinging loosely in a standing frame, was introduced in the late years of the eighteenth century,[1] and Sheraton illustrates an example in the *Drawing Book* (1791–4) which is fitted with small toilet boxes attached to the standards. The framework usually consisted of turned bars; the uprights are framed into trestle feet and connected by a stretcher (Figs. 58 and 244). A cheval glass appears in Gillow's Cost books under the name of a 'screen glass frame'. In the later Regency, the frame was sometimes of marked architectural character, being capped with a pediment, decorated in the centre with scrolling ornament.

In dressing glasses at the close of the eighteenth century an oblong plate took the place of the earlier shaping, and turning became the usual treatment. Alternatively, some glasses were suspended between lyre-shaped supports. Those without a box stand are like cheval glasses, and the frame consists usually of turned uprights finishing in trestle feet tied by a stretcher.

[1] The term *psyche* is said to be from Raphael's full-length painting of the fabled Psyche — *Dictionnaire de l'Académie* (1835).

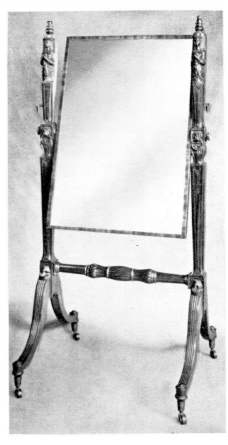

Fig. 244. Mahogany cheval glass; the standards headed by Egyptian terminal figures. c. 1810. Height, 5 ft 8½ in.; width, 2 ft 10 in.

Fig. 245. Lady's dressing-table of mahogany. The drawers are 'sham': the top, hinged at the back, lifts up to disclose in the centre an elaborately fitted interior; dressing slides at the ends pull out to uncover deep compartments; a looking glass is attached to the underside of the top. Adapted from a design by Sheraton (Encyclopaedia, Plate 47) for a sofa-writing table. c. 1805.

Fig. 246. (*Left*) *Satinwood dressing-table and dressing glass, banded with rosewood. Made by George Oakley for Papworth Hall in 1810. Height (including mirror), 5 ft; width, 4 ft 6 in.*

Fig. 247. (*Above*) *Mahogany dressing-table, inlaid with ebony stars and stringing lines. The drawers, made without handles, are activated by means of spring catches. From a design, dated 1805, in George Smith's* Household Furniture *(1808). See Fig. 30. Height, 2 ft 4 in.; length, 3 ft 10 in.; depth, 2 ft.*

In dressing mirrors resting upon a box stand this was simplified in treatment, and the drawers fitted with bone or ivory knob handles. The stand is sometimes supported on bone or ivory knob-feet. The frame surrounding the plate is frequently of convex section in the early nineteenth century.

DRESSING-TABLES
The dressing-table with a box lid or a lifting top enclosing dressing fittings continued to be made in the last years of the eighteenth, and was developed in the early nineteenth century (Fig. 245). Larger dressing-tables, however, fitted with drawers and having a movable dressing glass placed on the top, were then more usual. A satinwood table on turned legs, joined by a platform (Fig. 246), made by George Oakley in 1810, is characteristic of this type. Fig. 247 corresponds closely, apart from the form of the feet, with a design by Smith and his directions for the making of this piece have been carefully observed. Fig. 248, which is strongly influenced by French models, is in the 'Grecian style' of the second decade of the century. In later dressing-tables the glass is often a fixture.

Fig. 248. (*Left*) *Rosewood dressing-table and glass; the table mounted with French ormolu classical heads and having applied brass mouldings to the frieze.* c. 1815. *Height, 5 ft 6½ in.; width, 2 ft 7 in.*

Fig. 249. (*Right*) *Plan for the furnishing of a large drawing-room, submitted to a client by Gillow's in 1819. Gillow's, although 'first-grade manufacturers', were said to be deficient 'in inventiveness and style'. However, neo-rococo elements are already present at this date in their designs for some articles: Victorian production is foreshadowed in the form of the single chair standing to the right of the pier-table and in one of the armchairs; the supports of sofas and chairs, and of the centre table, are thick and heavily carved.*

Records of Furniture Makers

ADAIR, William, of 26 Wardour Street, Soho, carver and gilder, appears as one of the Royal tradesmen between 1799–1805. Adair supplied three pairs of large sofas and '3 small sofas to go between the windows' of the Great Saloon at the Queen's House (Buckingham Palace) in 1799 [H. Clifford Smith, *Buckingham Palace* (1931), p. 92].

BAILEY, *see* Tatham.

BECKWITH, Samuel, of 101 St Martin's Lane, partner in the firm of France and Beckwith, employed by the crown until the early years of the nineteenth century. The firm is included in the list of Master Cabinet-makers working in and about London in 1803, at the end of Sheraton's *Cabinet Dictionary*.

BLADES, John, of 5 Ludgate Hill, glass manufacturer, for whom, in 1816 and many subsequent years, John Papworth made designs [Wyatt Papworth, *John B. Papworth* (1879), pp. 37–8].

BOGAERT, Frederick (d. before 1826), a carver, born in the Low Countries, employed by Thomas Hope for furniture at Deepdene and his London house. Frederick Boeges, cabinet-maker, claimed £6 9s. for work done for the Prince Regent in 1795. In Holden's *London Directory* (1809–11) the firm is described as 'Bogaerts & Co., carvers and gilders, 23 Air Street, Piccadilly'. In George Smith's *Guide* (1828), Bogaert is spoken of as a carver who was also 'equally happy in his designs for furniture and other branches of interior decoration'.

BOILEAU, John James, of Sloane Square, a French painter and decorator employed at Carlton House (1783–9). He is mentioned as one of the French craftsmen and decorators brought to England by Sheringham of Great Marlborough Street [Wyatt Papworth, *John B. Papworth* (1879), p. 11]. He is described by George Smith, in his *Guide* (1828), as having a 'light, an airy and classic style of design for household articles of comfort', and as unsurpassed in his designs for ornamental plates or articles for casting in ormolu (p. 194).

BUHL, John, of St Martin's Lane, brazier, claimed in 1795 for braziery goods ordered and delivered at Carlton House.

BULLOCK, George, of 4 Tenterden Street, Hanover Square, sculptor, marble mason, furniture manufacturer and designer. He came to London about 1813–14, from Liverpool, where he had been established in business from 1805, or earlier. (A President of the Liverpool Academy 1810–11, he had exhibited as a sculptor at the Royal Academy, London, from 1804.) In London, from 1816 he contributed a number of designs for furniture to the (monthly) numbers of Ackermann's *Repository of Arts* (Brian Reade, *Regency Antiques*, 1953). Some characteristics of his style are apparent from the *Repository* comment

on his first plate — a design for a cabinet and window curtains: 'the cabinet', it is stated, 'is designed for execution in our native woods, relieved by metal ornaments; a style happily introduced both in respect of taste and true patriotism'. Bullock's style is eccentric and to some extent foreshadows Victorian taste. His work is described in Richard Brown's *Rudiments* (1820): 'The late Mr Bullock', writes Brown, 'was the only person who ventured into a new path: though some of his designs were certainly too massy and ponderous, nevertheless grandeur cannot be obtained without it; such are the standards to his octagon tables. There was great novelty without absurdity, as well as a happy relief, in his ornaments: yet many of his articles were considerably overcharged with buhl; sometimes the buhl-work was sunk in brass, and on other occasions the counterpart was of the same wood as the furniture itself, and the whole surface presented a brazen front. . . . Most of his ornaments were selected from British plants, and his woods were of English growth, which were admirably well polished. He has shewn that we need not roam to foreign climes for beautiful ornaments, but that we have abundance of plants and flowers equal to the Grecian, which, if adopted, would be found as pleasing as the antique.' It is curious that Bullock (whose insular temper appears decided) should have adopted a fashionable French technique. He was responsible for supplying chimney-pieces and some furniture to Sir Walter Scott for Abbotsford, 1816–18 [Clifford Musgrave, *Regency Furniture*, (1961), p. 81].

BUTLER, Thomas, of Catherine Street, '8 doors from the Strand', upholsterer, cabinet-maker and chair manufacturer; 'Patent bedstead maker to the King and Queen and Royal Family'; supplied articles of furniture 'particularly adapted for travelling and exportation'. A rival and near neighbour of Morgan and Sanders (*q.v.*), whose stock was of much the same character.

CAMPBELL, Robert, of Marylebone Street, Golden Square, upholsterer and cabinet-maker, patronised by the Prince of Wales and the Duke of York. He supplied furniture for Carlton House to the amount of £10,000 [H. Clifford Smith, *Buckingham Palace* (1931), p. 104]. Sheraton in his *Drawing Book* (1791–4) writes that 'two designs of library steps were taken from steps made by Mr Campbell, upholsterer to the Prince of Wales, and first made for the King'.

CHIPPENDALE, Thomas, the younger (1749–1822) (the eldest child of Thomas Chippendale, the well-known furniture-maker), carried on business at 60 St Martin's Lane after his father's death in 1779, trading as 'Chippendale & Haig', until partnership was dissolved in 1796 and Haig withdrew from the firm. He was made bankrupt in 1804, when his stock, sold at auction, included 'many articles of great taste and of the finest workmanship'. He visited Paris early in the nineteenth century, and a small sketch-book (formerly in the Bernal collection) is inscribed: 'sketches by Tho. Chippendale at various times'. These include ornament, chandeliers, and Empire furniture sketched in Paris and in the palace at Versailles.

From bills at Stourhead dating between 1795 and 1820 a number of pieces have been identified as the firm's workmanship for Sir Richard Colt Hoare, and extracts have been printed in the *Dictionary of English Furniture* ('Chippendale, Thomas, jun.') (Figs. 34, 78, 86 and 133). The influence of French design is seen in the Stourhead furniture, *e.g.* the writing chair [*Dictionary of English Furniture* (revised ed., 1954), Vol. I, p. 310] is very similar to a chair by Jean Antoine Bruns, illustrated in Salverte, *Les Ebénistes du XVIIIe siècle*, Plate viii. In 1819 Chippendale supplied furniture for Lord Townshend at Raynham. A letter quoted in C. Simon, from Lord Townshend, informs Chippendale that £1,200 has been placed to his account 'in payment of work done'.

George Smith, in his *Guide* (1828), speaks of Chippendale (lately deceased), known only amongst a few, 'as possessing a very great degree of taste with great ability as a draughtsman and designer'. He was a painter and had exhibited at the R.A. between 1784 and 1801.

COCKERILL, James, of 1–3 Curtain Road, Finsbury Square (workshop) and 203 Oxford Street. One of a number of London 'Japan Chair manufacturers' supplying painted and japanned furniture (drawing-room chairs 'in colours or black and gold', bedroom chairs to match bed-furniture, paper hangings etc., 'bed-cornishes', card tables).

DECAIX (or De Caiz), Alexis, a French metal worker, mentioned in Hope's *Household Furniture* (p. 10) as having executed (with Bogaert) 'the more complicated and enriched portions' of his furniture. De Caiz's name, 'manufacturer of bronzes, 43 Old Bond Street and 15 Rupert Street,' appears in Holden's *London Directory* (1809–11).

DAGUERRE, Dominique, a furniture dealer *à la Couronne d'Or* in the Rue St Honoré, Paris, where he sold, besides furniture, porcelain, glass, jewellery and *toutes sortes de curiosités*. He is mentioned in D'Oberkirch's *Memoirs* (May 25, 1784) as having at his shop a fine sideboard, which was to be sent to the Duke of Northumberland. Daguerre retired from business in the spring of 1793 (Salverte, *Les Ebénistes du XVIIIe siècle*, p. 75) and came to London. He claimed £15,500 for himself and for his partner Lignereux of Sloane Street, for furniture sold to the Prince of Wales and delivered to Carlton House in the proceedings of the Commissioners for the Prince of Wales's debts (1795). Furniture supplied by him has been identified at Buckingham Palace [*see* H. Clifford Smith, *Buckingham Palace* (1931), Plates 169 and 170].

DOMINIQUE (Dominic), Jean, of Marshall Street, gilder and brass founder, who executed work in ormolu for Carlton House between 1783 and 1786 [H. Clifford Smith, *Buckingham Palace* (1931), p. 103]. He claimed a small sum of £13 17s. 6d. for work at Carlton House in the proceedings of the Commissioners for the Prince of Wales's debts (1795).

ELLIOTT, Charles (1752–1832), 'Upholder to his Majesty, Patentee of Fracture bedstead' and cabinet-maker, of New Bond Street. His name occurs in the Royal Household Accounts, 1784–1810. Much furniture was supplied by the firm for William Tufnell at Langleys between 1797 and 1798 (*Country Life*, August 7, 1942). The firm appears at 97 New Bond Street until 1808, and subsequently at No. 104, under various styles (*Country Life*, January 23, 1942).

FOLGHAM, John, of 81 Fleet Street. Recorded as early as about 1760 as a 'shagreen case-maker' in Wood Street, 'opposite the Castle Inn'. 'Folqham, cabinet-maker' appears in the account of Samuel Whitbread, for Southill. The firm is styled 'Folgham and Son' case and cabinet-makers in 1803.

FRANCE, Edward, *see* Beckwith.

GAUBERT, Guillaume, of Panton Street, 'maker of ornamental furniture' claimed £1,133 19s. 8d. 'for ornaments at Carlton House' in 1795. When Horace Walpole visited Carlton House in 1785 he attributed the decorations to 'Gobert'.

GEE, John, of 49 Wardour Street, 'Turner and Chair maker to His Majesty'; he appears on the list of Master Cabinet-makers in the *Cabinet Dictionary* (1803), and in the *Post Office Directory*, 1817 (Figs. 91 and 93).

GILLOW, the firm of (of Lancaster and London), founded by Robert Gillow, a carpenter who about 1695 moved to Lancaster from Kirkham-in-the-Fylde, and was in 1728 made a Freeman of Lancaster. In 1757 Richard (1734–1811) the eldest son of Robert Gillow (1703–73), was taken into partnership, and subsequently his brothers, Robert and Thomas. About 1765 land was leased and premises built on a London site, in a newly fashionable quarter ('176 Oxford Road'). In 1790 the firm was styled 'Robert Gillow & Co., upholders', and in 1807 'G. and R. Gillow & Co., merchants, cabinet-makers, etc.' Not many years later the Gillows ceased to be connected with the business, though it was still carried on under their name. Richard Gillow (d. 1811), who in 1800 took out a patent for an improved dining-table, did much to extend and consolidate the business. His son, Richard Thomas Gillow, retired from the business in 1830.[1] Clark, in his *Historical and Descriptive Account of Lancaster* (1807), writes that the town had 'long been famous for the great quantities of mahogany furniture which have been made in it for home use and exportation. Mr Gillow's extensive warerooms, stored with every article of useful and ornamental mahogany furniture, are well worth the attention of the stranger, as they are said to be the best stocked of any in this line out of the metropolis'. A German visitor to London speaks (in 1807) of George and Richard Gillow as 'first-grade salesmen and manufacturers in London . . . their work is good and solid, though not of the first class in inventiveness and style'[2] (Figs. 94, 130 and 249). Among furniture bearing the stamp of the firm is a gilt couch in the Victoria and Albert Museum (Fig. 108).

HERVE, Francis, of 32 Lower John Street, Tottenham Court Road (*Universal British Directory*, 1790–3), 'French chairmaker', appears among the craftsmen employed at Carlton House between 1783 and 1786, the amount of his bill being £1,275 17s. 7d. (H. Clifford Smith, *Buckingham Palace* (1931), p. 103). The total estimate of his work amounted in 1789 to

---

[1] Gillow's, *A Record of a furnishing firm During Two Centuries* (1901).
[2] P. A. Nemmich, *Neueste Reise durch England* (1807).

£3,000 (*Ibid.*). In a bill from him at Althorp he charges Lady Spencer:

		£	s	d
1789.	'To a fauteuil à la Raine in wenscott.'	£2	3	6
1791.	'To six Cabriole Backstools [chairs] made to match a canopy Bedstead @ £2 7 6'	14	5	0
	'To two tête-à-tête to match @ £3 13'	7	6	0

A combined table and set of library steps in the Victoria and Albert Museum, dating from about 1790, bears his label. He was active as late as 1796.

INCE AND MAYHEW, a firm which ranked high among the cabinet-makers of the second half of the eighteenth century. The name of William Ince, cabinet-maker, appears among the subscribers to the *Director* (1754). The name of the firm is well known because of the existence of their *Universal System of Household Furniture*, published in parts between 1759 and 1763. Their address on the title page is Broad Street, Soho. In the *London Directories* 'Ince & Mayhew' are first mentioned in Broad Street in 1778, being described as 'cabinet-makers, upholsterers and dealers in Plate Glass'. By 1784 the firm had moved to Marshall Street, Carnaby Market, where they remained until the early nineteenth century. In the *Universal British Directory* (1803) the number is given as 47, and in Holden's *London Directory* (1809–11) as 48 Marshall Street. Mayhew, who survived Ince, died in 1811. A set of 18 mahogany chairs by the firm were supplied in 1793 to the Westminster Fire Office, and are still in the possession of this Company.

JENKINS, John, of 75 Long Acre, upholsterer. Inherited the traditions of the firm of Vile and Cobb, who were leading cabinet-makers in the mid-eighteenth century. 'Late foreman to Mr Cobb' and formerly partner of Strickland, 'nephew to the late Mr Vile'.

LE GAIGNEUR, Louis Constantin, owner of the 'Buhl Manufactury', 19 Queen Street, Edgware Road. Le Gaigneur, a Frenchman, who had perhaps transferred his workshop to London as a result of the Revolution, supplied pieces of Boulle furniture to the Prince Regent for Carlton House in 1815–16. There exists an account for £250 (Carlton House Ledger) for 'a buhl library table', perhaps one of a pair, now at Windsor Castle. A table of the same form as these, and signed, is in the Wallace Collection (Fig. 68).

LICHFIELD (or Litchfield), with Graham as partner appears in *London Directories* at 15 St Martin's Lane, 1783–4; and subsequently, 1790–3, at 72 St Martin's Lane. The partners subscribed to Sheraton's *Cabinet Dictionary* (1803). Payment to Lichfield, Morell and Co. is entered in the Southill accounts in 1798; and to Graham, upholsterer in 1808.

MARSH, William, of Mount Street, upholder and cabinet-maker, appears in the *London Directory* (1778). Some furniture at Southill, Bedfordshire, is stated in a letter of the Rev. Samuel Johnes (written in 1800) to be by Marsh, whose 'cabinets are superb', and who had 'made some frames for the glasses with a large bead that has a very good effect on the gilding' (Margaret Jourdain, *Decoration and Furniture of the Late Georgian Period*, p. 217). A portion of a mirror with a large bead in Mrs Whitbread's boudoir is illustrated in *Country Life*, December 7, 1929, p. 844. In the proceedings of

the Commissioners for the Prince of Wales's debts (1795), the firm is described as 'William Marsh & Co., upholders'. In 1802 the firm's style is Elward, Marsh & Tatham. (*See* Tatham.)

At Southill, Marsh worked probably from Holland's designs, or from designs made in his office.

(Figs. 2, 9, 72–3 and 102).

McLEAN. The name of John McLean, cabinet-maker, appears in the Westminster *Poll Book* (October, 1774). He issued a trade card on which his name is rendered 'Jas. Macklane, cabinet, chair-maker and upholsterer in Little Newport Street near Leicester Square'. A later trade card, which was issued from Upper Marylebone Street, indicates that he specialised in 'Elegant Parisian furniture' (Banks Collection, British Museum). The name of 'McLean & Son, Upper Terrace, Tottenham Court Road and 34 Marylebone Street', appears on the list of Master Cabinet-makers in the *Cabinet Dictionary* (1803), where the design for a work table is said to be 'taken from one executed by Mr M'Lean . . . who finishes these small articles in the neatest manner'. The *London Directories* (1809–14) give the name of 'John McLean & Son, upholders', at 58 Upper Marylebone Street, and after 1814 the firm's style is 'William McLean' (see letter from Sir Ambrose Heal, *Country Life*, September 3, 1943, p. 430). A cabinet bearing McLean's label is in the Victoria and Albert Museum (Murray Collection) and shows a number of brass mounts (Fig. 187).

MOREL, Nicholas, of Tenterden Street, cabinet-maker, is first mentioned in the accounts of the Commissioners for the Prince of Wales's debts (1795), in which he submitted a claim for £192. In 1802 he was established at 13 Great Marlborough Street. In Holden's *London Directory* (1809–11) the firm's style is 'Morel & Hughes, upholsterers and cabinet-makers' (Fig. 98). In the accounts preserved at Southill, £2,167 4s. 3d. was paid in 1798 to 'Lichfield, Morell & Co.' and in 1800, £1,580 7s. 5d. was paid to 'Morell, Marsh, etc.' In 1804 £306 was paid to 'Morell, etc., upholsterers' and £550 11s. 2d. in 1805. Small sums were paid to the firm in 1806 and 1807. In Ackermann's *Repository of Arts* (1825) mention is made of 'magnificent furniture' recently made for the Duke of Northumberland by Morel & Hughes. Morel later joined the firm of Seddon, and in the *London Directory* of 1832 the name appears as 'Seddon, Morel & Seddon'. (*See* Seddon.)

MORGAN AND SANDERS, a large manufacturing firm of considerable importance which was established in 1801 and by 1809 had executed 'very extensive orders for a vast variety of furniture'. An illustration of their showrooms in Catherine Street, the Strand, appears in Ackermann's *Repository of Arts* (August, 1809). They were then employing 'nearly one hundred mechanics [workmen], besides other necessary servants' with 'above ten times as many' outworkers 'in different parts of London and its environs'. The firm named their manufactory Trafalgar House after Nelson's victory. They are described as 'sofa, bed, and chair manufacturers, upholsterers and cabinet-makers, 15, 16 and 17, Catherine Street', in the *Post Office Directory*, 1815. Their stock included 'patent sofa-beds, chair-beds, brass screw four-posts and tent bedsteads, newly invented Imperial dining-tables, portable chairs, Trafalgar sideboard and dining-tables, Pitt's cabinet globe writing-table, and numberless other articles' (Figs. 200–201).

OAKLEY. The *Journal des Luxus und der Moden* (in 1801) speaks of 'everyone of taste and discrimination making their purchases at Oakley's, the most tasteful of London's cabinet-makers'; and in 1807 a German visitor writes that Oakley & Co. 'have not such far-reaching business [as the firm of Gillow], but they are the best-known for articles in the latest taste. Their warehouse is one of the sights of London' (P. A. Nemmich, *Neueste Reise durch England*, 1807).

George Oakley, upholsterer and cabinet-maker of 22 St Paul's Churchyard, first appears in the *London Directories* in 1790, and continues at that address until 1795. In 1796 the firm is styled 'Oakley & Kettle', at the same address; in 1799, 'George Oakley'; and in 1800, 'Oakley, Shackleton & Evans, 8 Old Bond Street and St Paul's Churchyard' (Shackleton had been formerly a partner in Seddon's).

The partners subscribed to Sheraton's *Cabinet Dictionary* (1803), and are recorded in Holden's *London Directory* (1809–1811).

From a manuscript inventory of the furniture supplied in 1810 for Papworth Hall, Cambridgeshire, a number of pieces (inherited by Mrs Stileman) can be identified (*Architectural Review*, 'English Empire Furniture made by George Oakley') (Figs. 134, 145, 157 and 246). The following extracts from this account include the more important pieces:

'An elegant satinwood winged wardrobe fitted with drawers and clothes shelves, and enclosed with panelled doors, formed of choice woods and elaborately inlaid with ebony.'	£75		
'The mahogany winged library case in the Grecian style, the door fitted with brass trellis wire and quilled silk curtains, with best locks and keys.'	£47	5	
'A capital mahogany sideboard supported on a stand, reeded legs and carved and bronzed paw feet with antique bronze heads.'	£26		
'A calamanderwood circular loo table upon pedestal and claws, the top inlaid with a border of stars in brass and ebony.'	£31	10	6

OLIVE AND ELKINS, of Charterhouse Square, cabinet and chair makers. 'W. Olive' contributed the majority of the plates contained in the *London Chair-makers' and Carvers' Book of Prices for Workmanship* (eds. 1802, 1808, 1823).

PARKER, of 8 Fleet Street, glass manufacturers, a firm founded by William Parker in 1756. In 1804 the firm's style was 'Perry & Parker', and in that year they corresponded with Sir Roger Newdigate about chandeliers supplied by them in 1788. The name changed to 'Perry & Co.' in 1817, when the business was transferred to 78 New Bond Street. The firm, which was prominent during the Regency period, making fine and very expensive 'lustres' and lighting fittings, flourished until a comparatively recent date, and possessed a large and invaluable collection of drawings for chandeliers dating from about 1790 until the accession of George IV, together with the names of their clients and the prices paid. Perry & Parker supplied numerous magnificent chandeliers to Carlton House, from 1789 (including one of 56 lights made in 1808 for 1,000 guineas) and to the Royal Pavilion, at Brighton. Among

numerous clients were Sir Roger Newdigate (1804) and the Emperor of China (1811).

PARKER, Thomas, of 18 Air Street, Piccadilly, a cabinet-maker who specialised in 'English Buhl' furniture. He was later (by 1823) at 22 Warwick Street, Golden Square.

PERRY, *see* Parker.

ROBINS, John, of Warwick Street, Golden Square; supplied furniture for the Bank of England in the early years of the nineteenth century. (Bolton, *Sir John Soane's Museum*, p. 133.)

RUSSELL, John, joiner and chair-maker, who was established in New Bond Street between 1776 and 1810; was chair-maker to the King (*Kent's Directory* and the *Universal British Directory*). In 1800 he supplied St James's Palace with 6 mahogany chair-frames with carved vase and feather backs, moulded feet to match, £9 18s. He supplied to the Prince Regent in 1808:

'a double-headed couch bedstead richly carved with figures and ornamented Egyptian heads, gilt leaves, chased honeysuckles, lyres.'	£209 10

Quoted in *The Burlington Magazine*, November, 1915 (vol. 28, p. 79).

SEDDON, a large and very important firm of furniture-makers, founded by George Seddon (a son of John Seddon of Blakelea and Eccles in Lancashire), who was born in 1727 and apprenticed in 1743 in London to George Clemaphon, of Cripplegate. He subsequently set up in business himself as cabinet-maker at London House (a disused palace of the Bishops of London) in Aldersgate.[1] His name appears in 1754 among the subscribers to Chippendale's *Director*. In *Kent's Directory* (1768) his address is given as 158 Aldersgate Street, but in the 1770–84 editions of this directory the number is given as 151 (the former premises having been destroyed by fire in 1768, when damage resulted to the amount of £7,300). Seddon was then employing about 80 workmen. After 1784, the address is 150 Aldersgate Street (the change again necessitated by a workshop fire). In 1785 he seems to have taken his son, also named George, into partnership, and the firm's style appears as 'George Seddon & Son'. This was changed in 1789 to 'George Seddon & Sons'. The business was by this date extremely prosperous, with stock valued (shortly before a third fire, which occurred in 1790) at about £119,000 — the equivalent perhaps of about £2,000,000 at the present day.

A German visitor to London in 1786 thus describes the firm: 'He employs four hundred apprentices on any work connected with the making of household furniture — joiners, carvers, gilders, mirror-workers, upholsterers, girdlers — who mould the bronze into graceful patterns — and locksmiths. All these are housed in a building with six wings. In the basement mirrors are cast and cut. Some other department contains nothing but chairs, sofas and stools of every description, some quite simple, others exquisitely carved and made of all varieties of wood, and one large room is full up with all the finished articles in this line, while others are occupied by writing-tables, cupboards, chests of drawers, charmingly fashioned desks, chests, both large and small, work and toilet tables in all manner of woods and patterns, from the simplest and cheapest to the most elegant and expensive. . . . Seddon, foster-father to four

[1] Seddon, *Memoirs and Letters of the late Thomas Seddon* (1858), p. 2.

hundred employees, seemed to me a respectable man, a man of genius too. . . . [He] has appreciated the value of all his own people's labour and toil and is for ever creating new forms.'[1]

In a description of Mr William Bingham's house in Philadelphia (1794), the drawing-room chairs are described as 'from Seddon's in London, of the newest taste, the back in the form of a lyre'.

From 1793 to 1800 the firm's style is 'George Seddon, Sons, & Shackleton',[2] subsequently reverting to 'Seddon & Sons' on the death of the first George Seddon, in 1801; in 1804 the firm changed its name to 'Thomas and George Seddon'. Thomas, the senior partner, dying in 1804, his name drops out of the directories, and the business is carried on under the name of George Seddon (Fig. 131). In 1816 and 1817 George Seddon and Thomas (his nephew) are given as tenants of 150 Moorgate Street; on the death of the senior partner, George, in 1818, the name of Thomas Seddon only appears. From 1820 to 1836 Thomas and George (his younger brother) were at 149–150 Aldersgate Street, and in 1826 they opened a West End branch at 16 Lower Grosvenor Street, where they were joined by Nicholas Morel (q.v.). In 1832 the directory gives the style of the firm as 'Seddon, Morel & Seddon'. In the following year Thomas and George Seddon opened premises in Gray's Inn Road to which, in 1837, they transferred their business.

Between 1826 and 1830 Morel & Seddon supplied upwards of £200,000 worth of furniture for Windsor Castle [H. Clifford Smith, *Buckingham Palace* (1931), p. 159 note, and *Country Life*, October 21, 1933] (Figs. 97, 99 and 100). The account was investigated after George IV's death, and the firm received only £179,300, signing the last receipt, November 12, 1831.

SEMPLE, J. and A., proprietors of Semple's Upholstery Warehouse, of 2 Berners Street (transferred from 78 Margaret Street about 1805) (Figs. 135–6).

SHERATON, Thomas (1751–1806). Most of what is known of Thomas Sheraton is based chiefly on scant information from his works. He was born in humble circumstances at Stockton-on-Tees. He is first heard of not as a designer or craftsman, but as a Baptist, and on the title-page of his book, *A Scriptural Illustration of the Doctrine of Regeneration* (1782), he describes himself as 'a mechanic, and one who never received the advantages of a *collegial* or *academical* education'. In 1791–4 he issued the *Cabinet-Maker and Upholsterer's Drawing-Book* (which passed through two subsequent editions), containing some 113 copperplates. A *Cabinet Dictionary* published in 1803 is illustrated with 88 copperplates, and contains a list of 252 cabinet-makers in and about London; of his last work, the *Cabinet-Maker, Upholsterer, and General Artists' Encyclopaedia*, 30 of the projected 125 parts were published between 1804 and 1806. His trade card, which gives his address as 106 Wardour Street, Soho, states that he 'teaches Perspective, Architecture and Ornaments, makes Designs for Cabinet-makers' (*see* Fig. 136). He died at Broad Street, Soho, in 1806, and the *Gentleman's Magazine*, in an obituary notice, states that he had been for 'many years a journeyman cabinet-maker; but since the year 1793 . . . has supported himself by his exertions as an author' (Figs. 23–5 and 170).

[1] *Sophie in London* (*1786*) (1933), pp. 173–5.
[2] The new partner, Thomas Shackleton, had married Mary Seddon.

SMITH, George, cabinet-maker and designer, who published in 1808 (being then in business in Princes Street, Cavendish Square) a *Collection of Designs for Household Furniture and Interior Decoration*, with 'Preliminary Remarks', in which he speaks of the recent 'propitious change' in furniture design which has 'arisen from a more close investigation and imitation of the beautiful remains of ancient sculpture and painting'. He tells us that his designs were 'studied from the best antique examples of the Egyptian, Greek and Roman styles' but specimens in the Gothic (Figs. 46 and 49) and Chinese tastes are added. A chair with lion-head terminals (Fig. 81) and a dressing-table (Fig. 247) correspond with designs in his book. In 1812 he issued a *Collection of Ornamental Designs* 'after the manner of the antique' (in which the 'purest antique ornament' is 'accommodated to modern embellishment'). The collection consists chiefly of ornamental *motifs* for the metal worker, carver and statuary, but there are two designs for pedestals, a tripod and a chair 'after the antique'. His *Cabinet-Maker's and Upholsterer's Guide* (1828) was issued from Brewer Street, Golden Square. In this work he writes that he has had an experience of forty years, both in the theory and practice of cabinet-making, and has been patronised by George IV and received testimonies from Thomas Hope, and describes himself as 'upholsterer and furniture draughtsman to his Majesty and principal of the drawing Academy, Brewer Street, Golden Square'. In the preface he writes that his *Household Furniture* (1808) has become wholly obsolete by the change of taste during the last twenty years.

(Figs. 27, 29–30, 63–4 and 219).

SNELL, William, of 15 Hanover Street, Long Acre, upholsterer; appears on the list of Master Cabinet-makers in the *Cabinet Dictionary* (1803). By 1817 in partnership with Edward Snell, and by 1822 (in Albemarle Street) recorded as specialising in the production of furniture made after current French models.

STUBBS, John, proprietor of Chair 'Manufactory', in the City Road and in Brick Lane, Old Street, 'for all Sorts of Yew Tree, Gothic and Windsor Chairs, Alcoves and Rural Seats, Garden Machines [invalid chairs], Dyed Chairs etc.' He appears on the list of Master Cabinet-makers in the *Cabinet Dictionary* (1803).

TAITT, Richard, of 92 Jermyn Street, St James's, upholsterer and joiner, appears in the *London Directories* in 1788 and continues until 1800; became one of the Royal tradesmen in 1793 (Lord Chamberlain's accounts, P.R.O.).

TAITT, John, of 75 Swallow Street, Piccadilly, upholsterer and cabinet-maker, first appears in the *London Directories* at this address in 1779, and continues there until 1785, when he moves to 254 Oxford Street, where he remains until 1799. [He is listed among the Royal tradesmen in H. Clifford Smith, *Buckingham Palace* (1931), p. 277.]

TATHAM, Thomas, of 13 Mount Street, was the eldest son of Ralph Tatham (d. 1779) and brother of the architect, Charles Heathcote Tatham. He joined the firm of William Marsh of Mount Street, from 1795 the principal cabinet-makers to George, Prince of Wales. Tatham became head of the firm of Marsh & Tatham in 1809, and shortly afterwards the firm's style was 'Tatham and Bailey, upholsterers to his Royal Highness the Prince of Wales, of 14 Mount Street' (Holden's *London Directory*, 1809–11). The sum of £1,695 10s. 3d. was paid to 'upholsterer, Tatham, etc.', in 1801 in the Southill accounts, and a further sum £3,737 15s. 5d. is entered in 1802 as paid to 'Tatham, Morell, etc.' In 1809 £1,120 9s. 10d. is paid to Tatham and in the following year £1,162 13s. 5d. In 1811, £1,154 9s. 3d. is entered in the firm's account, and in 1812 £1,070 11s. 9d. In 1811 the firm was 'Tatham, Bailey & Saunders'; and, in 1817, 'Bailey and Saunders'. Thomas Tatham died in 1818 at Brighton, leaving an estate to the value of £60,000 (*Gentleman's Magazine*, Jan., 1818).

(Figs. 8, 11–12 and 212).

TAYLOR, John Richard, of 16 Bedford Court, Covent Garden, designer and upholsterer. Said to have been with Oakley's (*q.v.*) until about 1820. Subsequently at Covent Garden; during the 1820's contributed a number of plates to Ackermann's *Repository of Arts*. About 1825 he published two small volumes of his designs for furniture and drapery, *The Upholsterer's and Cabinet Maker's Pocket Assistant* (Fig. 60).

VULLIAMY. A well-known firm founded by Justin Vulliamy, partner of Benjamin Gray, who obtained the appointment of clockmaker to the Crown in 1742. In 1786, a German visitor, who paid a visit to Vulliamy's, 'witnessed works of exquisite beauty and perfection there. It is no prejudice on my part to state that no Paris invention comes up to those which I saw here; and truly, ideas for practical use cannot be more nobly represented' [*Sophie in London, 1786* (1933), p. 100]. Benjamin Lewis Vulliamy (1780–1854), third in succession of this famous family, introduced several peculiarities and improvements into the clocks made by the firm. He was made free of the Clockmaker's Company in 1809, admitted to the Livery in 1810, and five times filled the office of Master. 'He was a man of refined taste in art, and possessed no small knowledge of architecture, painting and engraving.' Benjamin Lewis Vulliamy from 1806 onwards was employed by the Prince of Wales not only on the repairing and making of clocks, but on the making and repair of metal work, mounts and objects of all kinds [H. Clifford Smith, *Buckingham Palace* (1931), p. 113]. A pair of candelabra at Harewood House, having ormolu candle-branches springing from a black marble column mounted with lion masks, and resting on a base of ormolu and ebony, is signed 'Vulliamy, London, 1811'.

WEBB, William, near the Turnpike, Newington, 'Maker of Yew Tree, Gothic and Windsor chairs, China and Rural Seats', etc.; succeeded by 'R. Webb', and later 'Webb and Bruce', of Kings Road, Chelsea, and at Hammersmith; active about 1820.

SHORT BIBLIOGRAPHY

C. H. TATHAM
Etchings, representing the best examples of Ancient Ornamental Architecture . . . 1799; 2nd edition, 1803; 3rd edition, 1810.

THOMAS SHERATON
The Cabinet Dictionary, 1803.
The Cabinet-Maker, Upholsterer and General Artist's Encyclopaedia, 1804–6.

THOMAS HOPE
Household Furniture and Interior Decoration, 1807.

GEORGE SMITH
A Collection of Designs for Household Furniture and Interior Decoration, 1808.

R. ACKERMANN (Editor)
The Repository of Arts, Literature, Commerce, 1809–28.

RICHARD BROWN
The Rudiments of Drawing Cabinet and Upholstery Furniture . . . after the manner of the antique, 1820; 2nd edition, 1822; reprinted, 1835.

PETER AND M. A. NICHOLSON
The Practical Cabinet Maker, Upholsterer and Complete Decorator, 1826–7; the plates reprinted, c. 1835.

GEORGE SMITH
The Cabinet-Maker and Upholsterer's Guide, 1828.

J. C. LOUDON
An Encyclopaedia of Cottage, Farm and Villa Architecture and Furniture, 1833; reprinted 1835, 1847 and 1857.

———

RALPH EDWARDS
Article in *The Burlington Magazine*, 'The last phase of "Regency" design', Vol. lxxi, number 417 (Dec. 1937).

THERLE HUGHES
Article in *Antiques Review*, 'Furniture design of the Regency', number 2 (1949).

BRIAN READE
Regency Antiques, Batsford, 1953.

JOHN HARRIS
Regency Furniture Designs 1803–1826, Tiranti, 1961.

CLIFFORD MUSGRAVE
Regency Furniture 1800 to 1830, Faber and Faber, 1961.

Index

Marjorie F. Crick.